MznLnx

Missing Links Exam Preps

Exam Prep for

Essentials of Management

DuBrin, 8th Edition

The MznLnx Exam Prep is your link from the texbook and lecture to your exams.
The MznLnx Exam Preps are unauthorized and comprehensive reviews of your textbooks.

MznLnx

Rico
Publications

Exam Prep for Essentials of Management
8th Edition
DuBrin

Publisher: Raymond Houge
Assistant Editor: Michael Rouger
Text and Cover Designer: Lisa Buckner
Marketing Manager: Sara Swagger
Project Manager, Editorial Production: Jerry Emerson
Art Director: Vernon Lowerui

Product Manager: Dave Mason
Editorial Assitant: Rachel Guzmanji
Pedagogy: Debra Long
Cover Image: Jim Reed/Getty Images
Text and Cover Printer: City Printing, Inc.
Compositor: Media Mix, Inc.

For more information about our products, contact us at:
Dave.Mason@RicoPublications.com

For permission to use material from this text or product, submit a request online to:
Dave.Mason@RicoPublications.com

Printed in the United States
ISBN:

Contents

TO THE STUDENT

COMPREHENSIVE

The *MznLnx* Exam Prep series is designed to help you pass your exams. Editors at MznLnx review your textbooks and then prepare these practice exams to help you master the textbook material. Unlike study guides, workbooks, and practice tests provided by the texbook publisher and textbook authors, *MznLnx* gives you ***all*** of the material in each chapter in exam form, not just samples, so you can be sure to nail your exam.

MECHANICAL

The MznLnx Exam Prep series creates exams that will help you learn the subject matter as well as test you on your understanding. Each question is designed to help you master the concept. Just working through the exams, you gain an understanding of the subject--its a simple mechanical process that produces success.

INTEGRATED STUDY GUIDE AND REVIEW

MznLnx is not just a set of exams designed to test you, its also a comprehensive review of the subject content. Each exam question is also a review of the concept, making sure that you will get the answer correct without having to go to other sources of material. You learn as you go! Its the easiest way to pass an exam.

HUMOR

Studying can be tedious and dry. MznLnx's instructional design includes moderate humor within the exam questions on occassion, to break the tedium and revitalize the brain

1. _________ is one of the managerial functions like planning, organizing, staffing and directing. It is an important function because it helps to check the errors and to take the corrective action so that deviation from standards are minimized and stated goals of the organization are achieved in desired manner.According to modern concepts, _________ is a foreseeing action whereas earlier concept of _________ was used only when errors were detected. _________ in management means setting standards, measuring actual performance and taking corrective action.

a. Turnover
b. Decision tree pruning
c. Schedule of reinforcement
d. Control

2. In economics, business, retail, and accounting, a _________ is the value of money that has been used up to produce something, and hence is not available for use anymore. In economics, a _________ is an alternative that is given up as a result of a decision. In business, the _________ may be one of acquisition, in which case the amount of money expended to acquire it is counted as _________.

a. Fixed costs
b. Cost overrun
c. Cost allocation
d. Cost

3. _________ is the process whereby companies use cost accounting to report or control the various costs of doing business.

_________ generally describes the approaches and activities of managers in short run and long run planning and control decisions that increase value for customers and lower costs of products and services.

a. Genbutsu
b. Strict liability
c. Missing completely at random
d. Cost Management

4. _________ for short is a descriptive term for certain executives in a business operation. It is also a formal title held by some business executives, most commonly in the hospitality industry.

A _________ has broad, overall responsibility for a business or organization. Whereas a manager may be responsible for one functional area, the _________ is responsible for all areas.

a. Managing director
b. Chief knowledge officer
c. Chief technology officer
d. General manager

5. An _________ is a person who has possession of an enterprise and assumes significant accountability for the inherent risks and the outcome. It is an ambitious leader who combines land, labor, and capital to create and market new goods or services. The term is a loanword from French and was first defined by the Irish economist Richard Cantillon.
a. AAAI
b. A Stake in the Outcome
c. A4e
d. Entrepreneur

6. _________ is an increasingly broadening term with which an organization, or other human system describes the combination of traditionally administrative personnel functions with acquisition and application of skills, knowledge and experience, Employee Relations and resource planning at various levels. The field draws upon concepts developed in Industrial/Organizational Psychology and System Theory. _________ has at least two related interpretations depending on context. The original usage derives from political economy and economics, where it was traditionally called labor, one of four factors of production although this perspective is changing as a function of new and ongoing research into more strategic approaches at national levels. This first usage is used more in terms of '_________ development', and can go beyond just organizations to the level of nations . The more traditional usage within corporations and businesses refers to the individuals within a firm or agency, and to the portion of the organization that deals with hiring, firing, training, and other personnel issues, typically referred to as `_________ management'.
a. Progressive discipline
b. Bradford Factor
c. Human resource management
d. Human resources

7. A _________ is a list of the general tasks and responsibilities of a position. Typically, it also includes to whom the position reports, specifications such as the qualifications needed by the person in the job, salary range for the position, etc. A _________ is usually developed by conducting a job analysis, which includes examining the tasks and sequences of tasks necessary to perform the job.
a. Recruitment
b. Recruitment advertising
c. Job description
d. Recruitment Process Insourcing

8.

_________ is a commonly used, yet poorly defined concept in industrial and organizational psychology, the branch of psychology that deals with the workplace. It most commonly refers to whether a person performs their job well. Despite the confusion over how it should be exactly defined, performance is an extremely important criterion that relates to organizational outcomes and success.

a. 1990 Clean Air Act
b. 33 Strategies of War
c. 28-hour day
d. Job performance

9. _________ is subcontracting a process, such as product design or manufacturing, to a third-party company. The decision to outsource is often made in the interest of lowering cost or making better use of time and energy costs, redirecting or conserving energy directed at the competencies of a particular business, or to make more efficient use of land, labor, capital, (information) technology and resources. _________ became part of the business lexicon during the 1980s.

a. Operant conditioning
b. Unemployment insurance
c. Opinion leadership
d. Outsourcing

10. _________ has been described as the 'process of social influence in which one person can enlist the aid and support of others in the accomplishment of a common task' . A definition more inclusive of followers comes from Alan Keith of Genentech who said '_________ is ultimately about creating a way for people to contribute to making something extraordinary happen.'

_________ is one of the most salient aspects of the organizational context. However, defining _________ has been challenging.

a. Situational leadership
b. 1990 Clean Air Act
c. 28-hour day
d. Leadership

11. _________ is an organization's process of defining its strategy and making decisions on allocating its resources to pursue this strategy, including its capital and people. Various business analysis techniques can be used in _________, including SWOT analysis (Strengths, Weaknesses, Opportunities, and Threats) and PEST analysis (Political, Economic, Social, and Technological analysis) or STEER analysis involving Socio-cultural, Technological, Economic, Ecological, and Regulatory factors and EPISTEL (Environment, Political, Informatic, Social, Technological, Economic and Legal)

_________ is the formal consideration of an organization's future course. All _________ deals with at least one of three key questions:

1. 'What do we do?'
2. 'For whom do we do it?'
3. 'How do we excel?'

In business _________, the third question is better phrased 'How can we beat or avoid competition?'. (Bradford and Duncan, page 1.)

a. Strategic planning
b. 1990 Clean Air Act
c. 33 Strategies of War
d. 28-hour day

12. An _________ is a subset of strategic work plan. It describes short-term ways of achieving milestones and explains how, or what portion of, a strategic plan will be put into operation during a given operational period, in the case of commercial application, a fiscal year or another given budgetary term. An operational plan is the basis for, and justification of an annual operating budget request.

a. Operational planning
b. AAAI
c. A4e
d. A Stake in the Outcome

13. _________ is a strategic planning method used to evaluate the Strengths, Weaknesses, Opportunities, and Threats involved in a project or in a business venture. It involves specifying the objective of the business venture or project and identifying the internal and external factors that are favorable and unfavorable to achieving that objective. The technique is credited to Albert Humphrey, who led a convention at Stanford University in the 1960s and 1970s using data from Fortune 500 companies.

a. Market share
b. Marketing
c. Corporate image
d. SWOT analysis

14. In politics, a _________, (by metaphor with the carved _________ at the prow of a sailing ship), is a person who holds an important title or office yet executes little actual power, most commonly limited by convention rather than law. Common _________s include constitutional monarchs, such as: Queen Elizabeth II, the Emperor of Japan, or presidents in parliamentary democracies, such as the President of Israel.

While the authority of a _________ is in practice generally symbolic, public opinion, respect for the office or the office holder and access to high levels of government can give them significant influence on events.

a. Figurehead
b. 1990 Clean Air Act
c. 33 Strategies of War
d. 28-hour day

15. _________, widely known as F. W. Taylor, was an American mechanical engineer who sought to improve industrial efficiency. He is regarded as the father of scientific management, and was one of the first management consultants.

Taylor was one of the intellectual leaders of the Efficiency Movement and his ideas, broadly conceived, were highly influential in the Progressive Era.

a. Douglas N. Daft
b. Frederick Winslow Taylor
c. Geoffrey Colvin
d. Jonah Jacob Goldberg

16. '_________' refers to mental and communicative algorithms applied during social communications and interactions in order to reach certain effects or results. The term '_________' is used often in business contexts to refer to the measure of a person's ability to operate within business organizations through social communication and interactions. _________ are how people relate to one another.

a. A4e
b. A Stake in the Outcome
c. AAAI
d. Interpersonal skills

17. _________s is a sociological term for a person's 'EQ' (Emotional Intelligence Quotient), which refers to the cluster of personality traits, social graces, communication, language, personal habits, friendliness, and optimism that mark us. _________s complement hard skills (part of a person's IQ), which are the technical requirements of a job and many such similar jobs.

A person's _________ EQ is an important part of individual contribution to the success of an organization.

a. Social network analysis
b. Social awareness
c. Social influence
d. Soft skill

18. In economics, _________ refers to the ability of a person or a country to produce a particular good at a lower marginal cost and opportunity cost than another person or country. It is the ability to produce a product most efficiently given all the other products that could be produced. It can be contrasted with absolute advantage which refers to the ability of a person or a country to produce a particular good at a lower absolute cost than another.
a. 33 Strategies of War
b. 1990 Clean Air Act
c. 28-hour day
d. Comparative advantage

19. The _________ 1970 is an Act of the United Kingdom Parliament which prohibits any less favourable treatment between men and women in terms of pay and conditions of employment. It came into force on 29 December 1975. The term pay is interpreted in a broad sense to include, on top of wages, things like holidays, pension rights, company perks and some kinds of bonuses.
a. Oncale v. Sundowner Offshore Services
b. Australian labour law
c. Architectural Barriers Act of 1968
d. Equal Pay Act

20. A _________ is a type of bar chart that illustrates a project schedule. _________s illustrate the start and finish dates of the terminal elements and summary elements of a project. Terminal elements and summary elements comprise the work breakdown structure of the project.
a. 1990 Clean Air Act
b. Gantt chart
c. 33 Strategies of War
d. 28-hour day

21. _________ is an advertisement in which a particular product specifically mentions a competitor by name for the express purpose of showing why the competitor is inferior to the product naming it.

This should not be confused with parody advertisements, where a fictional product is being advertised for the purpose of poking fun at the particular advertisement, nor should it be confused with the use of a coined brand name for the purpose of comparing the product without actually naming an actual competitor. ('Wikipedia tastes better and is less filling than the Encyclopedia Galactica.')

In the 1980s, during what has been referred to as the cola wars, soft-drink manufacturer Pepsi ran a series of advertisements where people, caught on hidden camera, in a blind taste test, chose Pepsi over rival Coca-Cola.

a. 28-hour day
b. 33 Strategies of War
c. 1990 Clean Air Act
d. Comparative advertising

22. _________ is a theory of management that analyzes and synthesizes workflows, with the objective of improving labour productivity. The core ideas of the theory were developed by Frederick Winslow Taylor in the 1880s and 1890s, and were first published in his monographs, Shop Management and The Principles of _________ Taylor believed that decisions based upon tradition and rules of thumb should be replaced by precise procedures developed after careful study of an individual at work.
a. Value engineering
b. Capacity planning
c. Master production schedule
d. Scientific management

23. The _________ is a standardized, on-scene, all-hazard incident management concept. It is a management protocol originally designed for emergency management agencies in the United States which was later federalized there. It has since been adopted by agencies in other countries.
a. A Stake in the Outcome
b. AAAI
c. A4e
d. Incident Command Structure

24. _________ and Theory Y are theories of human motivation created and developed by Douglas McGregor at the MIT Sloan School of Management in the 1960s that have been used in human resource management, organizational behavior, organizational communication and organizational development. They describe two very different attitudes toward workforce motivation. McGregor felt that companies followed either one or the other approach.

In _________, which many managers practice, management assumes employees are inherently lazy and will avoid work if they can. They inherently dislike work. Because of this, workers need to be closely supervised and comprehensive systems of controls developed.

a. Management team
b. Cash cow
c. Job enrichment
d. Theory X

25. Theory X and _________ are theories of human motivation created and developed by Douglas McGregor at the MIT Sloan School of Management in the 1960s that have been used in human resource management, organizational behavior, organizational communication and organizational development. They describe two very different attitudes toward workforce motivation. McGregor felt that companies followed either one or the other approach.

In _________, management assumes employees may be ambitious and self-motivated and exercise self-control. It is believed that employees enjoy their mental and physical work duties.

a. Theory Y
b. Contingency theory
c. Business Workflow Analysis
d. Design leadership

26. The _________ is a form of reactivity whereby subjects improve an aspect of their behavior being experimentally measured simply in response to the fact that they are being studied, not in response to any particular experimental manipulation.

The term was coined in 1955 by Henry A. Landsberger when analyzing older experiments from 1924-1932 at the Hawthorne Works (outside Chicago.) Hawthorne Works had commissioned a study to see if its workers would become more productive in higher or lower levels of light.

a. Hawthorne effect
b. 33 Strategies of War
c. 1990 Clean Air Act
d. 28-hour day

27. The _________ refers to situations in which students perform better than other students simply because they are expected to do so. The effect is named after George Bernard Shaw's play Pygmalion, in which a professor makes a bet that he can teach a poor flower girl to speak and act like an upper-class lady, and is successful.

The _________ requires a student to internalize the expectations of their superiors.

a. Halo effect
b. Confirmation bias
c. Pygmalion effect
d. Distinction bias

28. _________ is the term used to describe a situation where different entities cooperate advantageously for a final outcome. Simply defined, it means that the whole is greater than the sum of the individual parts. Although the whole will be greater than each individual part, this is not the concept of _________.
a. 33 Strategies of War
b. 28-hour day
c. 1990 Clean Air Act
d. Synergy

1. The _________ is an international organization designed by its founders to supervise and liberalize international trade. The organization officially commenced on 1 January 1995, under the Marrakesh Agreement, succeeding the 1947 General Agreement on Tariffs and Trade (GATT.)

The _________ deals with regulation of trade between participating countries; it provides a framework for negotiating and formalising trade agreements, and a dispute resolution process aimed at enforcing participants' adherence to _________ agreements which are signed by representatives of member governments and ratified by their parliaments.

a. 1990 Clean Air Act
b. National Institute for Occupational Safety and Health
c. Network planning and design
d. World Trade Organization

2. _________ describes the relocation by a company of a business process from one country to another -- typically an operational process, such as manufacturing such as accounting. Even state governments employ _________.

The term is in use in several distinct but closely related ways.

a. AAAI
b. Offshoring
c. A4e
d. A Stake in the Outcome

3. The term '_________' refers to the concept of collecting information and attempting to spot a pattern in the information. In some fields of study, the term '_________' has more formally-defined meanings.

In project management _________ is a mathematical technique that uses historical results to predict future outcome.

a. Least squares
b. Trend analysis
c. Regression analysis
d. Stepwise regression

4. A _________ or transnational corporation is a corporation or enterprise that manages production or delivers services in more than one country. It can also be referred to as an international corporation.

The first modern _________ is generally thought to be the Dutch East India Company, established in 1602.

a. Command center
b. Small and medium enterprises
c. Financial Accounting Standards Board
d. Multinational corporation

5. _________ is subcontracting a process, such as product design or manufacturing, to a third-party company. The decision to outsource is often made in the interest of lowering cost or making better use of time and energy costs, redirecting or conserving energy directed at the competencies of a particular business, or to make more efficient use of land, labor, capital, (information) technology and resources. _________ became part of the business lexicon during the 1980s.
a. Opinion leadership
b. Unemployment insurance
c. Operant conditioning
d. Outsourcing

6. _________ is a type of trade policy that allows traders to act and transact without interference from government. Thus, the policy permits trading partners mutual gains from trade, with goods and services produced according to the theory of comparative advantage.

Under a _________ policy, prices are a reflection of true supply and demand, and are the sole determinant of resource allocation.

a. 1990 Clean Air Act
b. 28-hour day
c. 33 Strategies of War
d. Free Trade

7. _________ is a designated group of countries that have agreed to eliminate tariffs, quotas and preferences on most (if not all) goods and services traded between them. It can be considered the second stage of economic integration. Countries choose this kind of economic integration form if their economical structures are complementary.
a. Free trade area
b. 33 Strategies of War
c. 28-hour day
d. 1990 Clean Air Act

8. The _________ is a trilateral trade bloc in North America created by the governments of the United States, Canada, and Mexico. The agreement creating the trade bloc came into force on January 1, 1994. It superseded the Canada-United States Free Trade Agreement between the U.S. and Canada.

a. Career portfolios
b. North American Free Trade Agreement
c. Business war game
d. Trade union

9. _________ is a strategic planning method used to evaluate the Strengths, Weaknesses, Opportunities, and Threats involved in a project or in a business venture. It involves specifying the objective of the business venture or project and identifying the internal and external factors that are favorable and unfavorable to achieving that objective. The technique is credited to Albert Humphrey, who led a convention at Stanford University in the 1960s and 1970s using data from Fortune 500 companies.
a. Corporate image
b. SWOT analysis
c. Marketing
d. Market share

10. _________ has been described as the 'process of social influence in which one person can enlist the aid and support of others in the accomplishment of a common task' . A definition more inclusive of followers comes from Alan Keith of Genentech who said '_________ is ultimately about creating a way for people to contribute to making something extraordinary happen.'

_________ is one of the most salient aspects of the organizational context. However, defining _________ has been challenging.

a. Leadership
b. Situational leadership
c. 28-hour day
d. 1990 Clean Air Act

11. The _________ is the difference between the monetary value of exports and imports of output in an economy over a certain period of time. It is the relationship between a nation's imports and exports. A favourable _________ is known as a trade surplus and consists of exporting more than is imported; an unfavourable _________ is known as a trade deficit or, informally, a trade gap.
a. Balance of trade
b. Minimum wage
c. Deregulation
d. Value added

12. _________ are legal property rights over creations of the mind, both artistic and commercial, and the corresponding fields of law. Under _________ law, owners are granted certain exclusive rights to a variety of intangible assets, such as musical, literary, and artistic works; ideas, discoveries and inventions; and words, phrases, symbols, and designs. Common types of _________ include copyrights, trademarks, patents, industrial design rights and trade secrets.

a. Intellectual property
b. Unemployment Action Center
c. Equal Pay Act
d. Intent

13. _________ plant, and equipment, is a term used in accountancy for assets and property which cannot easily be converted into cash. This can be compared with current assets such as cash or bank accounts, which are described as liquid assets. In most cases, only tangible assets are referred to as fixed.

a. 1990 Clean Air Act
b. Fixed asset
c. 33 Strategies of War
d. 28-hour day

14. _________ is exchange of capital, goods, and services across international borders or territories. In most countries, it represents a significant share of gross domestic product (GDP.) While _________ has been present throughout much of history , its economic, social, and political importance has been on the rise in recent centuries.

a. International trade
b. AAAI
c. A4e
d. A Stake in the Outcome

15. _________ is the science, art and technology of enclosing or protecting products for distribution, storage, sale, and use. _________ also refers to the process of design, evaluation, and production of packages. _________ can be described as a coordinated system of preparing goods for transport, warehousing, logistics, sale, and end use.

a. Supply chain management
b. Supply chain
c. Wholesalers
d. Packaging

16. A _________ is an entity formed between two or more parties to undertake economic activity together. The parties agree to create a new entity by both contributing equity, and they then share in the revenues, expenses, and control of the enterprise. The venture can be for one specific project only, or a continuing business relationship such as the Fuji Xerox _________.

a. Patent
b. Meritor Savings Bank v. Vinson
c. Civil Rights Act of 1991
d. Joint venture

17. A _________ is a formal relationship between two or more parties to pursue a set of agreed upon goals or to meet a critical business need while remaining independent organizations.

Partners may provide the _________ with resources such as products, distribution channels, manufacturing capability, project funding, capital equipment, knowledge, expertise, or intellectual property. The alliance is a cooperation or collaboration which aims for a synergy where each partner hopes that the benefits from the alliance will be greater than those from individual efforts.

a. Process automation
b. Farmshoring
c. Golden parachute
d. Strategic alliance

18. An _________ is a person who has possession of an enterprise and assumes significant accountability for the inherent risks and the outcome. It is an ambitious leader who combines land, labor, and capital to create and market new goods or services. The term is a loanword from French and was first defined by the Irish economist Richard Cantillon.
a. A Stake in the Outcome
b. A4e
c. Entrepreneur
d. AAAI

19. The 'business case for _________', theorizes that in a global marketplace, a company that employs a diverse workforce (both men and women, people of many generations, people from ethnically and racially diverse backgrounds etc.) is better able to understand the demographics of the marketplace it serves and is thus better equipped to thrive in that marketplace than a company that has a more limited range of employee demographics.

An additional corollary suggests that a company that supports the _________ of its workforce can also improve employee satisfaction, productivity and retention.

a. Virtual team
b. Trademark
c. Kanban
d. Diversity

20. _________ in its literal sense is the process of transformation of local or regional phenomena into global ones. It can be described as a process by which the people of the world are unified into a single society and function together.

This process is a combination of economic, technological, sociocultural and political forces.

a. Cost Management
b. Histogram
c. Collaborative Planning, Forecasting and Replenishment
d. Globalization

21. A _________ or maquila is a factory that imports materials and equipment on a duty-free and tariff-free basis for assembly or manufacturing and then re-exports the assembled product, usually back to the originating country. A maquila is also referred to as a 'twin plant', or 'in-bond' industry. Nearly half a million Mexicans are employed in _________s.
a. 28-hour day
b. 33 Strategies of War
c. 1990 Clean Air Act
d. Maquiladora

22. _________ or _________ data refers to selected population characteristics as used in government, marketing or opinion research, or the _________ profiles used in such research. Note the distinction from the term 'demography' Commonly-used _________s include race, age, income, disabilities, mobility (in terms of travel time to work or number of vehicles available), educational attainment, home ownership, employment status, and even location.
a. Adam Smith
b. Abraham Harold Maslow
c. Demographic
d. Affiliation

23. _________ is, in very basic words, a position a firm occupies against its competitors.

According to Michael Porter, the three methods for creating a sustainable _________ are through:

1. Cost leadership

2. Differentiation

3. Focus (economics)

a. 1990 Clean Air Act
b. Theory Z
c. 28-hour day
d. Competitive advantage

24. _________ is training for the purpose of increasing participants' cultural awareness, knowledge, and skills, which is based on the assumption that the training will benefit an organization by protecting against civil rights violations, increasing the inclusion of different identity groups, and promoting better teamwork.

_________ has been a controversial issue, due to moral considerations as well as questioned efficiency or even counterproductivity.

According to Michael Bird, many project managers may feel that they are treading new territory as they lead project teams made of individuals from different cultures, heterogeneous mixes, and differing demographics.

a. Self-disclosure
b. Soft skill
c. Diversity training
d. Role conflict

1. The _________ 1970 is an Act of the United Kingdom Parliament which prohibits any less favourable treatment between men and women in terms of pay and conditions of employment. It came into force on 29 December 1975. The term pay is interpreted in a broad sense to include, on top of wages, things like holidays, pension rights, company perks and some kinds of bonuses.

a. Australian labour law
b. Equal Pay Act
c. Oncale v. Sundowner Offshore Services
d. Architectural Barriers Act of 1968

2. _________ is a form of applied ethics that examines ethical principles and moral or ethical problems that arise in a business environment. It applies to all aspects of business conduct and is relevant to the conduct of individuals and business organizations as a whole. Applied ethics is a field of ethics that deals with ethical questions in many fields such as medical, technical, legal and _________.

a. Hypernorms
b. Business ethics
c. Facilitation payments
d. Corporate Sustainability

3. A _________ occurs when an individual or organization (such as a policeman, lawyer, insurance adjuster, politician, engineer, executive, director of a corporation, medical research scientist, physician, writer, editor, or any other entrusted individual or organization) has an interest that might compromise their actions. The presence of a _________ is independent from the execution of impropriety.

In the legal profession, the duty of loyalty owed to a client prohibits an attorney (or a law firm) from representing any other party with interests adverse to those of a current client.

a. Conflict of interest
b. 28-hour day
c. Global Corruption Report
d. 1990 Clean Air Act

4. _________ is unwelcome harassment of a sexual nature, or based upon the receiving party's sex or gender. In some contexts or circumstances, _________ may be illegal. It includes a range of behavior from seemingly mild transgressions and annoyances to actual sexual abuse or sexual assault.

a. Hypernorms
b. 1990 Clean Air Act
c. Sexual harassment
d. 28-hour day

5. The _________ of 2002 (Pub.L. 107-204, 116 Stat. 745, enacted July 30, 2002), also known as the Public Company Accounting Reform and Investor Protection Act of 2002 and commonly called Sarbanes-Oxley, Sarbox or SOX, is a United States federal law enacted on July 30, 2002, as a reaction to a number of major corporate and accounting scandals including those affecting Enron, Tyco International, Adelphia, Peregrine Systems and WorldCom.

a. Letter of credit
b. Sarbanes-Oxley Act of 2002
c. Fair Labor Standards Act
d. Sarbanes-Oxley Act

6. Organizational culture is not the same as _________. It is wider and deeper concepts, something that an organization 'is' rather than what it 'has' (according to Buchanan and Huczynski.)

_________ is the total sum of the values, customs, traditions and meanings that make a company unique.

a. Job analysis
b. Corporate culture
c. Path-goal theory
d. Work design

7. _________ can be regarded as an outcome of mental processes (cognitive process) leading to the selection of a course of action among several alternatives. Every _________ process produces a final choice. The output can be an action or an opinion of choice.

a. 1990 Clean Air Act
b. 28-hour day
c. 33 Strategies of War
d. Decision making

8. _________ is a form of corporate self-regulation integrated into a business model. Ideally, _________ policy would function as a built-in, self-regulating mechanism whereby business would monitor and ensure their adherence to law, ethical standards, and international norms. Business would embrace responsibility for the impact of their activities on the environment, consumers, employees, communities, stakeholders and all other members of the public sphere.

a. 28-hour day
b. 33 Strategies of War
c. 1990 Clean Air Act
d. Corporate social responsibility

9. A mutual shareholder or _________ is an individual or company (including a corporation) that legally owns one or more shares of stock in a joint stock company. A company's shareholders collectively own that company. Thus, the typical goal of such companies is to enhance shareholder value.

a. Shareholder
b. Free riding
c. 1990 Clean Air Act
d. Stockholder

10. _________ refers to the movement of cash into or out of a business or financial product. It is usually measured during a specified, finite period of time. Measurement of _________ can be used

- to determine a project's rate of return or value. The time of _________s into and out of projects are used as inputs in financial models such as internal rate of return, and net present value.
- to determine problems with a business's liquidity. Being profitable does not necessarily mean being liquid. A company can fail because of a shortage of cash, even while profitable.
- as an alternate measure of a business's profits when it is believed that accrual accounting concepts do not represent economic realities. For example, a company may be notionally profitable but generating little operational cash (as may be the case for a company that barters its products rather than selling for cash.) In such a case, the company may be deriving additional operating cash by issuing shares evaluating default risk, re-investment requirements, etc.

_________ is a generic term used differently depending on the context. It may be defined by users for their own purposes.

a. Gross profit margin
b. Sweat equity
c. Gross profit
d. Cash flow

11. _________ is an advertisement in which a particular product specifically mentions a competitor by name for the express purpose of showing why the competitor is inferior to the product naming it.

This should not be confused with parody advertisements, where a fictional product is being advertised for the purpose of poking fun at the particular advertisement, nor should it be confused with the use of a coined brand name for the purpose of comparing the product without actually naming an actual competitor. ('Wikipedia tastes better and is less filling than the Encyclopedia Galactica.')

In the 1980s, during what has been referred to as the cola wars, soft-drink manufacturer Pepsi ran a series of advertisements where people, caught on hidden camera, in a blind taste test, chose Pepsi over rival Coca-Cola.

a. 33 Strategies of War
b. Comparative advertising
c. 1990 Clean Air Act
d. 28-hour day

12. _________ is a variable work schedule, in contrast to traditional work arrangements requiring employees to work a standard 9am to 5pm day. Under _________, there is typically a core period of the day when employees are expected to be at work (for example, between 11 am and 3pm), while the rest of the working day is 'flexitime', in which employees can choose when they work, subject to achieving total daily, weekly or monthly hours in the region of what the employer expects, and subject to the necessary work being done.

A _________ policy allows staff to determine when they will work, while a flexplace policy allows staff to determine where they will work.

a. Flextime
b. Bennett Amendment
c. Fiduciary
d. Certificate of Incorporation

13. _________ is a term used to describe the efforts made by a downsizing company to help its redundant employees through the redundancy transition and help them re-orientate to the job market . A consultancy firm usually provides the _________ services. This is achieved through practical and psychological support.

a. Outplacement
b. Unemployment Provision Convention, 1934
c. Unemployment compensation
d. Unemployment benefits

14. A _________ or a vicious circle (sometimes referred to as 'cycle' instead of 'circle') is a complex of events that reinforces itself through a feedback loop. A _________ has favorable results, and a vicious circle has detrimental results. A _________ can transform into a vicious circle if eventual negative feedback is ignored.

a. Power
b. Defined benefit pension plan
c. Virtuous circle
d. Fixed asset turnover

1. _________ is a strategic planning method used to evaluate the Strengths, Weaknesses, Opportunities, and Threats involved in a project or in a business venture. It involves specifying the objective of the business venture or project and identifying the internal and external factors that are favorable and unfavorable to achieving that objective. The technique is credited to Albert Humphrey, who led a convention at Stanford University in the 1960s and 1970s using data from Fortune 500 companies.

a. Corporate image
b. Market share
c. Marketing
d. SWOT analysis

2. _________ is an organization's process of defining its strategy and making decisions on allocating its resources to pursue this strategy, including its capital and people. Various business analysis techniques can be used in _________, including SWOT analysis (Strengths, Weaknesses, Opportunities, and Threats) and PEST analysis (Political, Economic, Social, and Technological analysis) or STEER analysis involving Socio-cultural, Technological, Economic, Ecological, and Regulatory factors and EPISTEL (Environment, Political, Informatic, Social, Technological, Economic and Legal)

_________ is the formal consideration of an organization's future course. All _________ deals with at least one of three key questions:

1. 'What do we do?'
2. 'For whom do we do it?'
3. 'How do we excel?'

In business _________, the third question is better phrased 'How can we beat or avoid competition?'. (Bradford and Duncan, page 1.)

a. Strategic planning
b. 28-hour day
c. 1990 Clean Air Act
d. 33 Strategies of War

3. An _________ is a subset of strategic work plan. It describes short-term ways of achieving milestones and explains how, or what portion of, a strategic plan will be put into operation during a given operational period, in the case of commercial application, a fiscal year or another given budgetary term. An operational plan is the basis for, and justification of an annual operating budget request.

a. Operational planning
b. A Stake in the Outcome
c. AAAI
d. A4e

4. The _________ refers to situations in which students perform better than other students simply because they are expected to do so. The effect is named after George Bernard Shaw's play Pygmalion, in which a professor makes a bet that he can teach a poor flower girl to speak and act like an upper-class lady, and is successful.

The _________ requires a student to internalize the expectations of their superiors.

a. Distinction bias
b. Confirmation bias
c. Halo effect
d. Pygmalion effect

5. A _________ is a plan devised for a specific situation when things could go wrong. _________s are often devised by governments or businesses who want to be prepared for anything that could happen. They are sometimes known as 'Back-up plans', 'Worst-case scenario plans' or 'Plan B'.

a. 28-hour day
b. 33 Strategies of War
c. 1990 Clean Air Act
d. Contingency plan

6. _________ is an advertisement in which a particular product specifically mentions a competitor by name for the express purpose of showing why the competitor is inferior to the product naming it.

This should not be confused with parody advertisements, where a fictional product is being advertised for the purpose of poking fun at the particular advertisement, nor should it be confused with the use of a coined brand name for the purpose of comparing the product without actually naming an actual competitor. ('Wikipedia tastes better and is less filling than the Encyclopedia Galactica.')

In the 1980s, during what has been referred to as the cola wars, soft-drink manufacturer Pepsi ran a series of advertisements where people, caught on hidden camera, in a blind taste test, chose Pepsi over rival Coca-Cola.

a. 33 Strategies of War
b. Comparative advertising
c. 28-hour day
d. 1990 Clean Air Act

7. A _________ is a formal relationship between two or more parties to pursue a set of agreed upon goals or to meet a critical business need while remaining independent organizations.

Partners may provide the _________ with resources such as products, distribution channels, manufacturing capability, project funding, capital equipment, knowledge, expertise, or intellectual property. The alliance is a cooperation or collaboration which aims for a synergy where each partner hopes that the benefits from the alliance will be greater than those from individual efforts.

a. Golden parachute
b. Farmshoring
c. Process automation
d. Strategic alliance

8. Procter is a surname, and may also refer to:

- Bryan Waller Procter (pseud. Barry Cornwall), English poet
- Goodwin Procter, American law firm
- _________, consumer products multinational

.

a. Downstream
b. Master and Servant Acts
c. Strict liability
d. Procter ' Gamble

9. _________ is something that a firm can do well and that meets the following three conditions:

Competencies are things that companys execute well across several business units or product sectors.

Firms usually have few competencies, but these are usually less liable to change rapidly.

1. It provides consumer benefits
2. It is not easy for competitors to imitate
3. It can be leveraged widely to many products and markets.

A _________ can take various forms, including technical/subject matter know-how, a reliable process and/or close relationships with customers and suppliers (Mascarenhas et al. 1998.)

a. Learning-by-doing
b. Core competency
c. NAIRU
d. Dominant Design

10. In marketing, _________ is the process of distinguishing the differences of a product or offering from others, to make it more attractive to a particular target market. This involves differentiating it from competitors' products as well as one's own product offerings.
a. PEST analysis
b. Market share
c. Market development
d. Product differentiation

11. The _________, 5 U.S.C. Â§ 552a, establishes a code of fair information practices that governs the collection, maintenance, use, and dissemination of personally identifiable information about individuals that is maintained in systems of records by federal agencies. A system of records is a group of records under the control of an agency from which information is retrieved by the name of the individual or by some identifier assigned to the individual.
a. Personal Responsibility and Work Opportunity Reconciliation Act
b. Privacy Act of 1974
c. No-FEAR Act
d. Negligence

12. _________ is a process of agreeing upon objectives within an organization so that management and employees agree to the objectives and understand what they are in the organization.

The term '_________' was first popularized by Peter Drucker in his 1954 book 'The Practice of Management'.

The essence of _________ is participative goal setting, choosing course of actions and decision making.

a. Business economics
b. Job enrichment
c. Clean sheet review
d. Management by objectives

13. _________ generally refers to a list of all planned expenses and revenues. It is a plan for saving and spending. A _________ is an important concept in microeconomics, which uses a _________ line to illustrate the trade-offs between two or more goods.

a. 33 Strategies of War
b. 28-hour day
c. Budget
d. 1990 Clean Air Act

14. _________ is, in very basic words, a position a firm occupies against its competitors.

According to Michael Porter, the three methods for creating a sustainable _________ are through:

1. Cost leadership

2. Differentiation

3. Focus (economics)

a. 1990 Clean Air Act
b. Competitive advantage
c. Theory Z
d. 28-hour day

1. The _________ is a decision making method for use among groups of many sizes, who want to make their decision quickly, as by a vote, but want everyone's opinions taken into account (as opposed to traditional voting, where only the largest group is considered) . The method of tallying is the difference. First, every member of the group gives their view of the solution, with a short explanation.

a. Hierarchical Decision Process
b. Belief decision matrix
c. Decision model
d. Nominal group technique

2. Procter is a surname, and may also refer to:

- Bryan Waller Procter (pseud. Barry Cornwall), English poet
- Goodwin Procter, American law firm
- _________, consumer products multinational

.

a. Strict liability
b. Master and Servant Acts
c. Downstream
d. Procter ' Gamble

3. _________ is a concept based on the fact that rationality of individuals is limited by the information they have, the cognitive limitations of their minds, and the finite amount of time they have to make decisions. This contrasts with the concept of rationality as optimization. Another way to look at _________ is that, because decision-makers lack the ability and resources to arrive at the optimal solution, they instead apply their rationality only after having greatly simplified the choices available.

a. Mixed strategy
b. Complete information
c. Bounded rationality
d. Transferable utility

4. _________ can be regarded as an outcome of mental processes (cognitive process) leading to the selection of a course of action among several alternatives. Every _________ process produces a final choice. The output can be an action or an opinion of choice.

a. 33 Strategies of War
b. 1990 Clean Air Act
c. 28-hour day
d. Decision making

5. The _________ of 2002 (Pub.L. 107-204, 116 Stat. 745, enacted July 30, 2002), also known as the Public Company Accounting Reform and Investor Protection Act of 2002 and commonly called Sarbanes-Oxley, Sarbox or SOX, is a United States federal law enacted on July 30, 2002, as a reaction to a number of major corporate and accounting scandals including those affecting Enron, Tyco International, Adelphia, Peregrine Systems and WorldCom.
   a. Sarbanes-Oxley Act of 2002
   b. Sarbanes-Oxley Act
   c. Letter of credit
   d. Fair Labor Standards Act

6. _________ is an adjective for experience-based techniques that help in problem solving, learning and discovery. A _________ method is particularly used to rapidly come to a solution that is hoped to be close to the best possible answer, or 'optimal solution'. _________s are 'rules of thumb', educated guesses, intuitive judgments or simply common sense.
   a. Heuristic
   b. Representativeness
   c. 1990 Clean Air Act
   d. 28-hour day

7. _________ , often measured as an _________ Quotient (EQ), is a term that describes the ability, capacity, skill or (in the case of the trait _________ model) a self-perceived ability, to identify, assess, and manage the emotions of one's self, of others, and of groups. Different models have been proposed for the definition of _________ and disagreement exists as to how the term should be used. Despite these disagreements, which are often highly technical, the ability _________ and trait _________ models (but not the mixed models) are enjoying considerable support in the literature and have successful applications in many different domains.
   a. Emotional intelligence
   b. A Stake in the Outcome
   c. A4e
   d. AAAI

8.

_________ is a commonly used, yet poorly defined concept in industrial and organizational psychology, the branch of psychology that deals with the workplace. It most commonly refers to whether a person performs their job well. Despite the confusion over how it should be exactly defined, performance is an extremely important criterion that relates to organizational outcomes and success.

a. 33 Strategies of War
b. 28-hour day
c. Job performance
d. 1990 Clean Air Act

9. Social consciousness is consciousness shared within a society. It can also be defined as _________; to be aware of the problems that different societies and communities face on a day-to-day basis; to be conscious of the difficulties and hardships of society.

There is debate as to exactly what the term means.

a. Self-disclosure
b. Soft skill
c. Role conflict
d. Social awareness

10. _________ is a type of trade policy that allows traders to act and transact without interference from government. Thus, the policy permits trading partners mutual gains from trade, with goods and services produced according to the theory of comparative advantage.

Under a _________ policy, prices are a reflection of true supply and demand, and are the sole determinant of resource allocation.

a. 33 Strategies of War
b. Free Trade
c. 28-hour day
d. 1990 Clean Air Act

11. _________ is a designated group of countries that have agreed to eliminate tariffs, quotas and preferences on most (if not all) goods and services traded between them. It can be considered the second stage of economic integration. Countries choose this kind of economic integration form if their economical structures are complementary.
a. 28-hour day
b. 33 Strategies of War
c. 1990 Clean Air Act
d. Free trade area

12. In decision theory and estimation theory, the _________ of an estimator, $\hat{\theta}$, of an unknown parameter of the distribution, θ, is the expected value of the loss function

$$R(\theta,\hat{\theta}) = \mathbb{E}_\theta L(\theta,\hat{\theta}) = \int L(\theta,\hat{\theta})\,dP_\theta.$$

where dP_θ is a probability measure parametrized by θ.

- For a scalar parameter θ and a quadratic loss function,

  $$L(\theta,\hat{\theta}) = (\theta - \hat{\theta})^2$$

  the _________ function becomes the mean squared error of the estimate,

  $$R(\theta,\hat{\theta}) = E_\theta(\theta - \hat{\theta})^2$$

- In density estimation, the unknown parameter is probability density itself. The loss function is typically chosen to be a norm in an appropriate function space. For example, for L^2 norm,

  $$L(f,\hat{f}) = \|f - \hat{f}\|_2^2$$

  the _________ function becomes the mean integrated squared error

  $$R(f,\hat{f}) = E\|f - \hat{f}\|^2$$

.

a. Risk
b. Linear model
c. Financial modeling
d. Risk aversion

13. The _________, 5 U.S.C. Â§ 552a, establishes a code of fair information practices that governs the collection, maintenance, use, and dissemination of personally identifiable information about individuals that is maintained in systems of records by federal agencies. A system of records is a group of records under the control of an agency from which information is retrieved by the name of the individual or by some identifier assigned to the individual.

a. Negligence
b. Privacy Act of 1974
c. Personal Responsibility and Work Opportunity Reconciliation Act
d. No-FEAR Act

14. _________ is a strategic planning method used to evaluate the Strengths, Weaknesses, Opportunities, and Threats involved in a project or in a business venture. It involves specifying the objective of the business venture or project and identifying the internal and external factors that are favorable and unfavorable to achieving that objective. The technique is credited to Albert Humphrey, who led a convention at Stanford University in the 1960s and 1970s using data from Fortune 500 companies.
a. Market share
b. Corporate image
c. SWOT analysis
d. Marketing

15. _________ is a type of thought exhibited by group members who try to minimize conflict and reach consensus without critically testing, analyzing, and evaluating ideas. Individual creativity, uniqueness, and independent thinking are lost in the pursuit of group cohesiveness, as are the advantages of reasonable balance in choice and thought that might normally be obtained by making decisions as a group. During _________, members of the group avoid promoting viewpoints outside the comfort zone of consensus thinking.
a. Psychological statistics
b. Self-report inventory
c. Groupthink
d. Diffusion of responsibility

16. _________ is a group creativity technique designed to generate a large number of ideas for the solution of a problem. The method was first popularized in the late 1930s by Alex Faickney Osborn in a book called Applied Imagination. Osborn proposed that groups could double their creative output with _________.
a. Brainstorming
b. Affiliation
c. Abraham Harold Maslow
d. Adam Smith

1. A _________ is a type of bar chart that illustrates a project schedule. _________s illustrate the start and finish dates of the terminal elements and summary elements of a project. Terminal elements and summary elements comprise the work breakdown structure of the project.

a. 33 Strategies of War
b. 1990 Clean Air Act
c. 28-hour day
d. Gantt chart

2. The _________ refers to situations in which students perform better than other students simply because they are expected to do so. The effect is named after George Bernard Shaw's play Pygmalion, in which a professor makes a bet that he can teach a poor flower girl to speak and act like an upper-class lady, and is successful.

The _________ requires a student to internalize the expectations of their superiors.

a. Pygmalion effect
b. Halo effect
c. Confirmation bias
d. Distinction bias

3. _________ is the process of estimation in unknown situations. Prediction is a similar, but more general term. Both can refer to estimation of time series, cross-sectional or longitudinal data.

a. 28-hour day
b. 1990 Clean Air Act
c. 33 Strategies of War
d. Forecasting

4. Procter is a surname, and may also refer to:

- Bryan Waller Procter (pseud. Barry Cornwall), English poet
- Goodwin Procter, American law firm
- _________, consumer products multinational

.

a. Master and Servant Acts
b. Downstream
c. Procter ' Gamble
d. Strict liability

5. _________, widely known as F. W. Taylor, was an American mechanical engineer who sought to improve industrial efficiency. He is regarded as the father of scientific management, and was one of the first management consultants.

Taylor was one of the intellectual leaders of the Efficiency Movement and his ideas, broadly conceived, were highly influential in the Progressive Era.

a. Douglas N. Daft
b. Jonah Jacob Goldberg
c. Geoffrey Colvin
d. Frederick Winslow Taylor

6. The Program (or Project) Evaluation and Review Technique, commonly abbreviated _________, is a model for project management designed to analyze and represent the tasks involved in completing a given project.

_________ is a method to analyze the involved tasks in completing a given project, specially the time needed to complete each task, and identifying the minimum time needed to complete the total project.

_________ was developed primarily to simplify the planning and scheduling of large and complex projects.

a. 28-hour day
b. 1990 Clean Air Act
c. PERT
d. 33 Strategies of War

7. A _________ is a decision support tool that uses a tree-like graph or model of decisions and their possible consequences, including chance event outcomes, resource costs, and utility. _________s are commonly used in operations research, specifically in decision analysis, to help identify a strategy most likely to reach a goal. Another use of _________s is as a descriptive means for calculating conditional probabilities.

a. Decision tree
b. 1990 Clean Air Act
c. 33 Strategies of War
d. 28-hour day

8. In probability theory and statistics, the _________ of a random variable is the integral of the random variable with respect to its probability measure. For discrete random variables this is equivalent to the probability-weighted sum of the possible values, and for continuous random variables with a density function it is the probability density -weighted integral of the possible values.

a. Expected value
b. A4e
c. A Stake in the Outcome
d. AAAI

9. _________ is an inventory strategy that strives to improve the return on investment of a business by reducing in-process inventory and its associated carrying costs. To meet _________ objectives, the process relies on signals between different points in the process. This means the process is often driven by a series of signals, or Kanban , which tell production when to make the next part. Kanban are usually 'tickets' but can be simple visual signals, such as the presence or absence of a part on a shelf. Implemented correctly, _________ can dramatically improve a manufacturing organization's return on investment, quality, and efficiency.
a. 33 Strategies of War
b. 28-hour day
c. 1990 Clean Air Act
d. Just-in-time

10. _________ is one of the managerial functions like planning, organizing, staffing and directing. It is an important function because it helps to check the errors and to take the corrective action so that deviation from standards are minimized and stated goals of the organization are achieved in desired manner.According to modern concepts, _________ is a foreseeing action whereas earlier concept of _________ was used only when errors were detected. _________ in management means setting standards, measuring actual performance and taking corrective action.
a. Control
b. Turnover
c. Decision tree pruning
d. Schedule of reinforcement

11. A _________ is a commercial building for storage of goods. _________s are used by manufacturers, importers, exporters, wholesalers, transport businesses, customs, etc. They are usually large plain buildings in industrial areas of cities and towns.
a. 1990 Clean Air Act
b. 33 Strategies of War
c. 28-hour day
d. Warehouse

12. The _________ states that, for many events, roughly 80% of the effects come from 20% of the causes. Business management thinker Joseph M. Juran suggested the principle and named it after Italian economist Vilfredo Pareto, who observed that 80% of the land in Italy was owned by 20% of the population. It is a common rule of thumb in business; e.g., '80% of your sales come from 20% of your clients.' Mathematically, where something is shared among a sufficiently large set of participants, there will always be a number k between 50 and 100 such that k% is taken by% of the participants.

a. Greenfield agreement

b. Bylaw

c. Board of directors

d. Pareto principle

1. _________ is a worldwide management consulting firm that focuses on solving issues of concern to senior management. McKinsey serves as an advisor to the world's leading businesses, governments, and institutions. It is widely recognized as a leader and one of the most prestigious firms in the management consulting industry.
   a. 28-hour day
   b. 1990 Clean Air Act
   c. 33 Strategies of War
   d. McKinsey ' Company

2. _________ is a strategic planning method used to evaluate the Strengths, Weaknesses, Opportunities, and Threats involved in a project or in a business venture. It involves specifying the objective of the business venture or project and identifying the internal and external factors that are favorable and unfavorable to achieving that objective. The technique is credited to Albert Humphrey, who led a convention at Stanford University in the 1960s and 1970s using data from Fortune 500 companies.
   a. Corporate image
   b. SWOT analysis
   c. Market share
   d. Marketing

3. A _________ is a list of the general tasks and responsibilities of a position. Typically, it also includes to whom the position reports, specifications such as the qualifications needed by the person in the job, salary range for the position, etc. A _________ is usually developed by conducting a job analysis, which includes examining the tasks and sequences of tasks necessary to perform the job.
   a. Recruitment Process Insourcing
   b. Recruitment advertising
   c. Recruitment
   d. Job description

4. In organizational development (OD), _________ is the application of Socio-Technical Systems principles and techniques to the humanization of work.

The aims of _________ to improved job satisfaction, to improved through-put, to improved quality and to reduced employee problems, e.g., grievances, absenteeism.

Under scientific management people would be directed by reason and the problems of industrial unrest would be appropriately (i.e., scientifically) addressed.

a. Graduate recruitment
b. Path-goal theory
c. Management process
d. Work design

5. _________ describes the situation when output from (or information about the result of) an event or phenomenon in the past will influence the same event/phenomenon in the present or future. When an event is part of a chain of cause-and-effect that forms a circuit or loop, then the event is said to 'feed back' into itself.

_________ is also a synonym for:

- _________ signal; the information about the initial event that is the basis for subsequent modification of the event.
- _________ loop; the causal path that leads from the initial generation of the _________ signal to the subsequent modification of the event.

_________ is a mechanism, process or signal that is looped back to control a system within itself. Such a loop is called a _________ loop.

a. Feedback loop
b. 1990 Clean Air Act
c. Positive feedback
d. Feedback

6.

_________ is a commonly used, yet poorly defined concept in industrial and organizational psychology, the branch of psychology that deals with the workplace. It most commonly refers to whether a person performs their job well. Despite the confusion over how it should be exactly defined, performance is an extremely important criterion that relates to organizational outcomes and success.

a. 33 Strategies of War
b. Job performance
c. 1990 Clean Air Act
d. 28-hour day

7. _________ is the change (processing) of information in any manner detectable by an observer. As such, it is a process which describes everything which happens (changes) in the universe, from the falling of a rock (a change in position) to the printing of a text file from a digital computer system. In the latter case, an information processor is changing the form of presentation of that text file.

a. A4e
b. AAAI
c. A Stake in the Outcome
d. Information processing

8. _________s is the science of designing the job, equipment, and workplace to fit the worker. Proper _________ design is necessary to prevent repetitive strain injuries, which can develop over time and can lead to long-term disability.

_________s is concerned with the 'fit' between people and their work.

a. Ergonomic
b. AAAI
c. A Stake in the Outcome
d. A4e

9. In economics, _________ is the desire to own something and the ability to pay for it. The term _________ signifies the ability or the willingness to buy a particular commodity at a given point of time.

a. 33 Strategies of War
b. 1990 Clean Air Act
c. 28-hour day
d. Demand

10. _________ is a dynamic of being mutually and physically responsible to and sharing a common set of principles with others. This concept differs distinctly from 'dependence' in that an interdependent relationship implies that all participants are emotionally, economically, ecologically and or morally 'interdependent.' Some people advocate freedom or independence as a sort of ultimate good; others do the same with devotion to one's family, community, or society. _________ recognizes the truth in each position and weaves them together.

a. Interdependence
b. A4e
c. AAAI
d. A Stake in the Outcome

11. _________ is the use of control systems (such as numerical control, programmable logic control, and other industrial control systems), in concert with other applications of information technology (such as computer-aided technologies [CAD, CAM, CAx]), to control industrial machinery and processes, reducing the need for human intervention. In the scope of industrialization, _________ is a step beyond mechanization. Whereas mechanization provided human operators with machinery to assist them with the physical requirements of work, _________ greatly reduces the need for human sensory and mental requirements as well.

a. AAAI
b. A4e
c. Automation
d. A Stake in the Outcome

12. _________ is an attempt to motivate employees by giving them the opportunity to use the range of their abilities. It is an idea that was developed by the American psychologist Frederick Herzberg in the 1950s. It can be contrasted to job enlargement which simply increases the number of tasks without changing the challenge.

a. Cash cow
b. Catfish effect
c. C-A-K-E
d. Job enrichment

13. _________ means increasing the scope of a job through extending the range of its job duties and responsibilities. This contradicts the principles of specialisation and the division of labour whereby work is divided into small units, each of which is performed repetitively by an individual worker. Some motivational theories suggest that the boredom and alienation caused by the division of labour can actually cause efficiency to fall.

a. Centralization
b. Mock interview
c. Job enlargement
d. Delayering

14. _________ is an approach to management development where an individual is moved through a schedule of assignments designed to give him or her a breadth of exposure to the entire operation.

_________ is also practiced to allow qualified employees to gain more insights into the processes of a company, and to reduce boredom and increase job satisfaction through job variation.

The term _________ can also mean the scheduled exchange of persons in offices, especially in public offices, prior to the end of incumbency or the legislative period.

a. 28-hour day
b. 1990 Clean Air Act
c. 33 Strategies of War
d. Job rotation

15. The _________ 1970 is an Act of the United Kingdom Parliament which prohibits any less favourable treatment between men and women in terms of pay and conditions of employment. It came into force on 29 December 1975. The term pay is interpreted in a broad sense to include, on top of wages, things like holidays, pension rights, company perks and some kinds of bonuses.

a. Oncale v. Sundowner Offshore Services
b. Australian labour law
c. Architectural Barriers Act of 1968
d. Equal Pay Act

16. _________ is a medical condition in which the median nerve is compressed at the wrist, leading to paresthesias, numbness and muscle weakness in the hand. The diagnosis of _________ is often misapplied to patients who have activity-related arm pain.

Most cases of _________ are idiopathic (without known cause); genetic factors determine most of the risk, and the role of arm use and other environmental factors is disputed.

a. 1990 Clean Air Act
b. Carpal tunnel syndrome
c. 28-hour day
d. 33 Strategies of War

17. _________ is a variable work schedule, in contrast to traditional work arrangements requiring employees to work a standard 9am to 5pm day. Under _________, there is typically a core period of the day when employees are expected to be at work (for example, between 11 am and 3pm), while the rest of the working day is 'flexitime', in which employees can choose when they work, subject to achieving total daily, weekly or monthly hours in the region of what the employer expects, and subject to the necessary work being done.

A _________ policy allows staff to determine when they will work, while a flexplace policy allows staff to determine where they will work.

a. Fiduciary
b. Certificate of Incorporation
c. Bennett Amendment
d. Flextime

18. _________ is an integrated communications-based process through which individuals and communities discover that existing and newly-identified needs and wants may be satisfied by the products and services of others.

_________ is defined by the American _________ Association as the activity, set of institutions, and processes for creating, communicating, delivering, and exchanging offerings that have value for customers, clients, partners, and society at large. The term developed from the original meaning which referred literally to going to market, as in shopping, or going to a market to buy or sell goods or services.

a. Customer relationship management
b. Disruptive technology
c. Market development
d. Marketing

19. _________ is an employment practice designed to make use of the 24 hours of the clock, rather than a standard working day. The term _________ includes both long-term night shifts and work schedules in which employees change or rotate shifts.

A related yet different concept, the work shift, is the time period during which a person is at work.

a. Labour law
b. Labor rights
c. Working time
d. Shift work

20. The legal _________ varies from nation to nation. The weekend is a part of the week usually lasting one or two days in which most paid workers do not work.

In Muslim-majority countries the legal work week in the Middle East is typically either Saturday through Wednesday , Saturday through Thursday or Sunday through Thursday as in Egypt.

a. Working Time Directive
b. Business day
c. Day One Christian Ministries
d. Workweek

21. _________, widely known as F. W. Taylor, was an American mechanical engineer who sought to improve industrial efficiency. He is regarded as the father of scientific management, and was one of the first management consultants.

Taylor was one of the intellectual leaders of the Efficiency Movement and his ideas, broadly conceived, were highly influential in the Progressive Era.

a. Douglas N. Daft
b. Geoffrey Colvin
c. Jonah Jacob Goldberg
d. Frederick Winslow Taylor

22. _________, e-commuting, e-work, telework, working from home (WFH), or working at home (WAH) is a work arrangement in which employees enjoy flexibility in working location and hours. In other words, the daily commute to a central place of work is replaced by telecommunication links. Many work from home, while others, occasionally also referred to as nomad workers or web commuters utilize mobile telecommunications technology to work from coffee shops or myriad other locations.

a. 28-hour day
b. 33 Strategies of War
c. Telecommuting
d. 1990 Clean Air Act

23. _________ is a method of supporting unassigned seating in an office environment. It is similar and is sometimes confused with hot desking, another method of supporting unassigned seating. _________ is reservation-based unassigned seating, whereas, hot desking is reservation-less unassigned seating.

a. 1990 Clean Air Act
b. 33 Strategies of War
c. 28-hour day
d. Hotelling

24. _________ is one of the managerial functions like planning, organizing, staffing and directing. It is an important function because it helps to check the errors and to take the corrective action so that deviation from standards are minimized and stated goals of the organization are achieved in desired manner.According to modern concepts, _________ is a foreseeing action whereas earlier concept of _________ was used only when errors were detected. _________ in management means setting standards, measuring actual performance and taking corrective action.

a. Decision tree pruning
b. Turnover
c. Schedule of reinforcement
d. Control

25. In economics, business, retail, and accounting, a _________ is the value of money that has been used up to produce something, and hence is not available for use anymore. In economics, a _________ is an alternative that is given up as a result of a decision. In business, the _________ may be one of acquisition, in which case the amount of money expended to acquire it is counted as _________.

a. Fixed costs
b. Cost allocation
c. Cost overrun
d. Cost

26. _________ is the process whereby companies use cost accounting to report or control the various costs of doing business.

_________ generally describes the approaches and activities of managers in short run and long run planning and control decisions that increase value for customers and lower costs of products and services.

a. Genbutsu
b. Strict liability
c. Missing completely at random
d. Cost Management

27. Processes and activities include everything that happens within the _________. The term processes and activities is used instead of the term business process because many _________s do not contain highly structured business processes involving a prescribed sequence of steps, each of which is triggered in a pre-defined manner. Such processes are sometimes described as 'artful processes' whose sequence and content 'depend on the skills, experience, and judgment of the primary actors.' (Hill et al., 2006) In effect, business process is but one of a number of different perspectives for analyzing the activities within a _________.

a. Skilled worker
b. Split shift
c. Work-at-home scheme
d. Work system

1. The _________ is the interlocking social structure that governs how people work together in practice. It is the aggregate of behaviors, interactions, norms, personal and professional connections through which work gets done and relationships are built among people who share a common organizational affiliation or cluster of affiliations. It consists of a dynamic set of personal relationships, social networks, communities of common interest, and emotional sources of motivation. The _________ evolves organically and spontaneously in response to changes in the work environment, the flux of people through its porous boundaries, and the complex social dynamics of its members.

a. Union shop
b. Open shop
c. Organizational effectiveness
d. Informal organization

2.

_________ is a commonly used, yet poorly defined concept in industrial and organizational psychology, the branch of psychology that deals with the workplace. It most commonly refers to whether a person performs their job well. Despite the confusion over how it should be exactly defined, performance is an extremely important criterion that relates to organizational outcomes and success.

a. 28-hour day
b. Job performance
c. 1990 Clean Air Act
d. 33 Strategies of War

3. _________ is an advertisement in which a particular product specifically mentions a competitor by name for the express purpose of showing why the competitor is inferior to the product naming it.

This should not be confused with parody advertisements, where a fictional product is being advertised for the purpose of poking fun at the particular advertisement, nor should it be confused with the use of a coined brand name for the purpose of comparing the product without actually naming an actual competitor. ('Wikipedia tastes better and is less filling than the Encyclopedia Galactica.')

In the 1980s, during what has been referred to as the cola wars, soft-drink manufacturer Pepsi ran a series of advertisements where people, caught on hidden camera, in a blind taste test, chose Pepsi over rival Coca-Cola.

a. 33 Strategies of War
b. 28-hour day
c. 1990 Clean Air Act
d. Comparative advertising

4. A _________ is a list of the general tasks and responsibilities of a position. Typically, it also includes to whom the position reports, specifications such as the qualifications needed by the person in the job, salary range for the position, etc. A _________ is usually developed by conducting a job analysis, which includes examining the tasks and sequences of tasks necessary to perform the job.

   a. Recruitment Process Insourcing
   b. Recruitment advertising
   c. Recruitment
   d. Job description

5. The _________ is a standardized, on-scene, all-hazard incident management concept. It is a management protocol originally designed for emergency management agencies in the United States which was later federalized there. It has since been adopted by agencies in other countries.

   a. AAAI
   b. A4e
   c. A Stake in the Outcome
   d. Incident Command Structure

6. _________ describes how content an individual is with his or her job.

The happier people are within their job, the more satisfied they are said to be. _________ is not the same as motivation, although it is clearly linked.

   a. Human relations
   b. Goal-setting theory
   c. Job analysis
   d. Job satisfaction

7. _________ refers to the process of grouping activities into departments.

Division of labour creates specialists who need coordination. This coordination is facilitated by grouping specialists together in departments.

   a. Departmentalization
   b. Division of labour
   c. Maximum wage
   d. Decent work

8. _________, widely known as F. W. Taylor, was an American mechanical engineer who sought to improve industrial efficiency. He is regarded as the father of scientific management, and was one of the first management consultants.

Taylor was one of the intellectual leaders of the Efficiency Movement and his ideas, broadly conceived, were highly influential in the Progressive Era.

a. Jonah Jacob Goldberg
b. Frederick Winslow Taylor
c. Douglas N. Daft
d. Geoffrey Colvin

9. Procter is a surname, and may also refer to:

- Bryan Waller Procter (pseud. Barry Cornwall), English poet
- Goodwin Procter, American law firm
- _________, consumer products multinational

a. Strict liability
b. Procter ' Gamble
c. Downstream
d. Master and Servant Acts

10. _________ is subcontracting a process, such as product design or manufacturing, to a third-party company. The decision to outsource is often made in the interest of lowering cost or making better use of time and energy costs, redirecting or conserving energy directed at the competencies of a particular business, or to make more efficient use of land, labor, capital, (information) technology and resources. _________ became part of the business lexicon during the 1980s.
a. Operant conditioning
b. Unemployment insurance
c. Outsourcing
d. Opinion leadership

11. _________(known as horizontal organization) refers to an organizational structure with few or no levels of intervening management between staff and managers. The idea is that well-trained workers will be more productive when they are more directly involved in the decision making process, rather than closely supervised by many layers of management.

This structure is generally possible only in smaller organizations or individual units within larger organizations.

a. 1990 Clean Air Act
b. 28-hour day
c. 33 Strategies of War
d. Flat organization

12. _________ is a type of organizational management in which people with similar skills are pooled for work assignments. For example, all engineers may be in one engineering department and report to an engineering manager, but these same engineers may be assigned to different projects and report to a project manager while working on that project. Therefore, each engineer may have to work under several managers to get their job done.
a. Span of control
b. Matrix management
c. Management development
d. Central Administration

13. _________ refers to the movement of cash into or out of a business or financial product. It is usually measured during a specified, finite period of time. Measurement of _________ can be used

- to determine a project's rate of return or value. The time of _________s into and out of projects are used as inputs in financial models such as internal rate of return, and net present value.
- to determine problems with a business's liquidity. Being profitable does not necessarily mean being liquid. A company can fail because of a shortage of cash, even while profitable.
- as an alternate measure of a business's profits when it is believed that accrual accounting concepts do not represent economic realities. For example, a company may be notionally profitable but generating little operational cash (as may be the case for a company that barters its products rather than selling for cash.) In such a case, the company may be deriving additional operating cash by issuing shares evaluating default risk, re-investment requirements, etc.

_________ is a generic term used differently depending on the context. It may be defined by users for their own purposes.

a. Gross profit
b. Cash flow
c. Sweat equity
d. Gross profit margin

14. _________ is a type of trade policy that allows traders to act and transact without interference from government. Thus, the policy permits trading partners mutual gains from trade, with goods and services produced according to the theory of comparative advantage.

Under a _________ policy, prices are a reflection of true supply and demand, and are the sole determinant of resource allocation.

a. 33 Strategies of War
b. Free Trade
c. 1990 Clean Air Act
d. 28-hour day

15. _________ is a designated group of countries that have agreed to eliminate tariffs, quotas and preferences on most (if not all) goods and services traded between them. It can be considered the second stage of economic integration. Countries choose this kind of economic integration form if their economical structures are complementary.
a. 1990 Clean Air Act
b. 28-hour day
c. 33 Strategies of War
d. Free trade area

16. In a military context, the _________ is the line of authority and responsibility along which orders are passed within a military unit and between different units. The term is also used in a civilian management context describing comparable hierarchical structures of authority.
a. 28-hour day
b. French leave
c. 1990 Clean Air Act
d. Chain of command

17. _________ is one of the managerial functions like planning, organizing, staffing and directing. It is an important function because it helps to check the errors and to take the corrective action so that deviation from standards are minimized and stated goals of the organization are achieved in desired manner.According to modern concepts, _________ is a foreseeing action whereas earlier concept of _________ was used only when errors were detected. _________ in management means setting standards, measuring actual performance and taking corrective action.
a. Turnover
b. Control
c. Decision tree pruning
d. Schedule of reinforcement

18. _________ is a term originating in military organization theory, but now used more commonly in business management, particularly human resource management. _________ refers to the number of subordinates a supervisor has.

In the hierarchical business organization of the past it was not uncommon to see average spans of 1 to 10 or even less. That is, one manager supervised ten employees on average.

a. Span of control
b. Mentoring
c. Senior management
d. CIFMS

19. _________ is an inventory strategy that strives to improve the return on investment of a business by reducing in-process inventory and its associated carrying costs. To meet _________ objectives, the process relies on signals between different points in the process. This means the process is often driven by a series of signals, or Kanban , which tell production when to make the next part. Kanban are usually 'tickets' but can be simple visual signals, such as the presence or absence of a part on a shelf. Implemented correctly, _________ can dramatically improve a manufacturing organization's return on investment, quality, and efficiency.
a. 33 Strategies of War
b. 28-hour day
c. Just-in-time
d. 1990 Clean Air Act

20. _________ (NYSE: DE) is an American corporation based in Moline, Illinois, and the leading manufacturer of agricultural machinery in the world. In 2008, it was listed as 102nd in the Fortune 500 ranking. Deere and Company agricultural products, usually sold under the John Deere name, include tractors, combine harvesters, balers, planters/seeders, ATVs and forestry equipment.
a. 33 Strategies of War
b. Deere ' Company
c. 28-hour day
d. 1990 Clean Air Act

21. _________ refers to increasing the spiritual, political, social or economic strength of individuals and communities. It often involves the empowered developing confidence in their own capacities.

The term Human _________ covers a vast landscape of meanings, interpretations, definitions and disciplines ranging from psychology and philosophy to the highly commercialized Self-Help industry and Motivational sciences.

a. AAAI
b. A4e
c. A Stake in the Outcome
d. Empowerment

22. _________ is the process by which the activities of an organisation, particularly those regarding decision-making, become concentrated within a particular location and/or group.

a. Product innovation
b. Chief operating officer
c. Corner office
d. Centralization

23. _________ is the process of dispersing decision-making governance closer to the people or citizen. It includes the dispersal of administration or governance in sectors or areas like engineering, management science, political science, political economy, sociology and economics. _________ is also possible in the dispersal of population and employment.

a. Business plan
b. Frenemy
c. Formula for Change
d. Decentralization

24. _________ is an idea in the field of Organizational studies and management which describes the psychology, attitudes, experiences, beliefs and Values (personal and cultural values) of an organization. It has been defined as 'the specific collection of values and norms that are shared by people and groups in an organization and that control the way they interact with each other and with stakeholders outside the organization.'

This definition continues to explain organizational values also known as 'beliefs and ideas about what kinds of goals members of an organization should pursue and ideas about the appropriate kinds or standards of behavior organizational members should use to achieve these goals. From organizational values develop organizational norms, guidelines or expectations that prescribe appropriate kinds of behavior by employees in particular situations and control the behavior of organizational members towards one another.'

_________ is not the same as corporate culture.

a. Union shop
b. Organizational development
c. Organizational effectiveness
d. Organizational culture

25. The 'business case for _________', theorizes that in a global marketplace, a company that employs a diverse workforce (both men and women, people of many generations, people from ethnically and racially diverse backgrounds etc.) is better able to understand the demographics of the marketplace it serves and is thus better equipped to thrive in that marketplace than a company that has a more limited range of employee demographics.

An additional corollary suggests that a company that supports the _________ of its workforce can also improve employee satisfaction, productivity and retention.

a. Trademark
b. Kanban
c. Virtual team
d. Diversity

26. In sociology, anthropology and cultural studies, a _________ is a group of people with a culture (whether distinct or hidden) which differentiates them from the larger culture to which they belong. If a particular _________ is characterized by a systematic opposition to the dominant culture, it may be described as a counterculture.

As early as 1950, David Riesman distinguished between a majority, 'which passively accepted commercially provided styles and meanings, and a '_________' which actively sought a minority style ...

a. 1990 Clean Air Act
b. 28-hour day
c. 33 Strategies of War
d. Subculture

27. _________ is the state or fact of exclusive rights and control over property, which may be an object, land/real estate or intellectual property. An _________ right is also referred to as title. The concept of _________ has existed for thousands of years and in all cultures.

a. Emanation of the state
b. A4e
c. A Stake in the Outcome
d. Ownership

28. _________ is a structured approach to transitioning individuals, teams, and organizations from a current state to a desired future state. The current definition of _________ includes both organizational _________ processes and individual _________ models, which together are used to manage the people side of change.

A number of models are available for understanding the transitioning of individuals through the phases of _________ and strengthening organizational development initiative in both government and corporate sectors.

a. 33 Strategies of War
b. Change management
c. 28-hour day
d. 1990 Clean Air Act

29. _________ is a business management strategy, initially implemented by Motorola, that today enjoys widespread application in many sectors of industry.

_________ seeks to improve the quality of process outputs by identifying and removing the causes of defects (errors) and variation in manufacturing and business processes. It uses a set of quality management methods, including statistical methods, and creates a special infrastructure of people within the organization ('Black Belts' etc.)

a. Takt time
b. Production line
c. Theory of constraints
d. Six sigma

1. _________ is a contract between two parties, one being the employer and the other being the employee. An employee may be defined as: 'A person in the service of another under any contract of hire, express or implied, oral or written, where the employer has the power or right to control and direct the employee in the material details of how the work is to be performed.' Black's Law Dictionary page 471 (5th ed. 1979.)

   a. Exit interview
   b. Employment
   c. Employment counsellor
   d. Employment rate

2. The term _________ was created by President Lyndon B. Johnson when he signed Executive Order 11246 on September 24, 1965, created to prohibit federal contractors from discriminating against employees on the basis of race, sex, creed, religion, color, or national origin. In more recent times, most employers have also added sexual orientation to the list of non-discrimination.

The Executive Order also required contractors to implement affirmative action plans to increase the participation of minorities and women in the workplace.

   a. A Stake in the Outcome
   b. Equal employment opportunity
   c. AAAI
   d. A4e

3. In a human resources context, _________ or labor _________ is the rate at which an employer gains and loses employees. Simple ways to describe it are 'how long employees tend to stay' or 'the rate of traffic through the revolving door.' _________ is measured for individual companies and for their industry as a whole. If an employer is said to have a high _________ relative to its competitors, it means that employees of that company have a shorter average tenure than those of other companies in the same industry.

   a. Career portfolios
   b. Continuous
   c. Ten year occupational employment projection
   d. Turnover

4.

The terms _________ and positive action refer to policies that take race, ethnicity, or gender into consideration in an attempt to promote equal opportunity. The focus of such policies ranges from employment and education to public contracting and health programs. The impetus towards _________ is twofold: to maximize diversity in all levels of society, along with its presumed benefits, and to redress perceived disadvantages due to overt, institutional, or involuntary discrimination.

a. Abraham Harold Maslow
b. Adam Smith
c. Affiliation
d. Affirmative action

5. The _________ of 1967, Pub. L. No. 90-202, 81 Stat. 602 (Dec. 15, 1967), codified as Chapter 14 of Title 29 of the United States Code, 29 U.S.C. Â§ 621 through 29 U.S.C. Â§ 634 (ADEA), prohibits employment discrimination against persons 40 years of age or older in the United States). The law also sets standards for pensions and benefits provided by employers and requires that information about the needs of older workers be provided to the general public.
a. Age Discrimination in Employment Act
b. Unemployment and Farm Relief Act
c. Extra time
d. Undue hardship

6. The _________ 1970 is an Act of the United Kingdom Parliament which prohibits any less favourable treatment between men and women in terms of pay and conditions of employment. It came into force on 29 December 1975. The term pay is interpreted in a broad sense to include, on top of wages, things like holidays, pension rights, company perks and some kinds of bonuses.
a. Oncale v. Sundowner Offshore Services
b. Architectural Barriers Act of 1968
c. Australian labour law
d. Equal Pay Act

7. The _________ refers to situations in which students perform better than other students simply because they are expected to do so. The effect is named after George Bernard Shaw's play Pygmalion, in which a professor makes a bet that he can teach a poor flower girl to speak and act like an upper-class lady, and is successful.

The _________ requires a student to internalize the expectations of their superiors.

a. Distinction bias
b. Pygmalion effect
c. Confirmation bias
d. Halo effect

8. A _________ is a formal statement of a set of business goals, the reasons why they are believed attainable, and the plan for reaching those goals. It may also contain background information about the organization or team attempting to reach those goals.

The business goals may be defined for for-profit or for non-profit organizations.

a. Distributed management
b. Business plan
c. Time management
d. Crisis management

9. _________ refers to the process of screening, and selecting qualified people for a job at an organization or firm mid- and large-size organizations and companies often retain professional recruiters or outsource some of the process to _________ agencies. External _________ is the process of attracting and selecting employees from outside the organization.

The _________ industry has four main types of agencies: employment agencies, _________ websites and job search engines, 'headhunters' for executive and professional _________, and in-house _________.

a. Labour hire
b. Referral recruitment
c. Recruitment Process Outsourcing
d. Recruitment

10. A _________ is a list of the general tasks and responsibilities of a position. Typically, it also includes to whom the position reports, specifications such as the qualifications needed by the person in the job, salary range for the position, etc. A _________ is usually developed by conducting a job analysis, which includes examining the tasks and sequences of tasks necessary to perform the job.

a. Recruitment
b. Recruitment advertising
c. Job description
d. Recruitment Process Insourcing

11. A _________ is a process in which a potential employee is evaluated by an employer for prospective employment in their company, organization and was established in the late 16th century.

A _________ typically precedes the hiring decision, and is used to evaluate the candidate. The interview is usually preceded by the evaluation of submitted résumés from interested candidates, then selecting a small number of candidates for interviews.

a. Split shift
b. Supported employment
c. Payrolling
d. Job interview

12. The term _________ in logic applies to arguments or statements.

An argument is valid if and only if the truth of its premises entails the truth of its conclusion, it would be self-contradictory to affirm the premises and deny the conclusion. The corresponding conditional of a valid argument is a logical truth and the negation of its corresponding conditional is a contradiction.

a. 1990 Clean Air Act
b. Fuzzy logic
c. Simplification
d. Validity

13. The _________, 5 U.S.C. Â§ 552a, establishes a code of fair information practices that governs the collection, maintenance, use, and dissemination of personally identifiable information about individuals that is maintained in systems of records by federal agencies. A system of records is a group of records under the control of an agency from which information is retrieved by the name of the individual or by some identifier assigned to the individual.
a. No-FEAR Act
b. Personal Responsibility and Work Opportunity Reconciliation Act
c. Negligence
d. Privacy Act of 1974

14. The _________ of 1990 (ADA) is the short title of United States (Pub.L. 101-336, 104 Stat. 327, enacted July 26, 1990), codified at 42 U.S.C. Â§ 12101 et seq. It was signed into law on July 26, 1990, by President George H. W. Bush, and later amended with changes effective January 1, 2009. The ADA is a wide-ranging civil rights law that prohibits, under certain circumstances, discrimination based on disability. It affords similar protections against discrimination to Americans with disabilities as the Civil Rights Act of 1964,
a. Equal Pay Act of 1963
b. Employment discrimination
c. Australian labour law
d. Americans with Disabilities Act

15. _________ is subcontracting a process, such as product design or manufacturing, to a third-party company. The decision to outsource is often made in the interest of lowering cost or making better use of time and energy costs, redirecting or conserving energy directed at the competencies of a particular business, or to make more efficient use of land, labor, capital, (information) technology and resources. _________ became part of the business lexicon during the 1980s.

a. Outsourcing
b. Opinion leadership
c. Unemployment insurance
d. Operant conditioning

16. _________ is one of five major domains of personality discovered by psychologists. Openness involves active imagination, aesthetic sensitivity, attentiveness to inner feelings, preference for variety, and intellectual curiosity. A great deal of psychometric research has demonstrated that these qualities are statistically correlated.

a. Openness to experience
b. Extraversion
c. Introversion
d. Introverts

17. _________ is a process for determining and addressing needs, or gaps between current conditions and desired conditions organizations it is known as community needs analysis. It involves identifying material problems/deficits/weaknesses and advantages/opportunites/strengths, and evaluating possible solutions that take those qualities into consideration.

a. 1990 Clean Air Act
b. 28-hour day
c. Needs assessment
d. 33 Strategies of War

18. _________ refers to various methodologies for analyzing the requirements of a job.

The general purpose of _________ is to document the requirements of a job and the work performed. Job and task analysis is performed as a basis for later improvements, including: definition of a job domain; describing a job; developing performance appraisals, selection systems, promotion criteria, training needs assessment, and compensation plans.

a. Work design
b. Job analysis
c. Management process
d. Hersey-Blanchard situational theory

19.

_________ is a commonly used, yet poorly defined concept in industrial and organizational psychology, the branch of psychology that deals with the workplace. It most commonly refers to whether a person performs their job well. Despite the confusion over how it should be exactly defined, performance is an extremely important criterion that relates to organizational outcomes and success.

a. Job performance
b. 28-hour day
c. 33 Strategies of War
d. 1990 Clean Air Act

20. _________ describes the situation when output from (or information about the result of) an event or phenomenon in the past will influence the same event/phenomenon in the present or future. When an event is part of a chain of cause-and-effect that forms a circuit or loop, then the event is said to 'feed back' into itself.

_________ is also a synonym for:

- _________ signal; the information about the initial event that is the basis for subsequent modification of the event.
- _________ loop; the causal path that leads from the initial generation of the _________ signal to the subsequent modification of the event.

_________ is a mechanism, process or signal that is looped back to control a system within itself. Such a loop is called a _________ loop.

a. Feedback loop
b. Feedback
c. 1990 Clean Air Act
d. Positive feedback

21. A _________ is a form of periodic payment from an employer to an employee, which may be specified in an employment contract. It is contrasted with piece wages, where each job, hour or other unit is paid separately, rather than on a periodic basis.

From the point of a view of running a business, _________ can also be viewed as the cost of acquiring human resources for running operations, and is then termed personnel expense or _________ expense.

a. Training and development
b. Human resource management
c. Human resources
d. Salary

22. A _________ is a compensation, usually financial, received by a worker in exchange for their labor.

Compensation in terms of _________s is given to worker and compensation in terms of salary is given to employees. Compensation is a monetary benefits given to employees in returns of the services provided by them.

a. Performance-related pay
b. Wage
c. State Compensation Insurance Fund
d. Profit-sharing agreement

23. _________ and benefits in kind are various non-wage compensations provided to employees in addition to their normal wages or salaries. Where an employee exchanges (cash) wages for some other form of benefit, this is generally referred to as a 'salary sacrifice' arrangement. In most countries, most kinds of _________ are taxable to at least some degree.
a. A Stake in the Outcome
b. A4e
c. Interactive Accommodation Process
d. Employee benefits

24. _________ is the strategic and coherent approach to the management of an organisation's most valued assets - the people working there who individually and collectively contribute to the achievement of the objectives of the business. The terms '_________' and 'human resources' (HR) have largely replaced the term 'personnel management' as a description of the processes involved in managing people in organizations. In simple sense, _________ means employing people, developing their resources, utilizing, maintaining and compensating their services in tune with the job and organizational requirement.
a. Revolving door syndrome
b. Progressive discipline
c. Job knowledge
d. Human resource management

25. A _________ or labor union is an organization of workers who have banded together to achieve common goals in key areas and working conditions. The _________, through its leadership, bargains with the employer on behalf of union members (rank and file members) and negotiates labor contracts (Collective bargaining) with employers. This may include the negotiation of wages, work rules, complaint procedures, rules governing hiring, firing and promotion of workers, benefits, workplace safety and policies.

a. Working time
b. Company union
c. Labour law
d. Trade union

1. _________ has been described as the 'process of social influence in which one person can enlist the aid and support of others in the accomplishment of a common task' . A definition more inclusive of followers comes from Alan Keith of Genentech who said '_________ is ultimately about creating a way for people to contribute to making something extraordinary happen.'

_________ is one of the most salient aspects of the organizational context. However, defining _________ has been challenging.

a. 28-hour day
b. Leadership
c. Situational leadership
d. 1990 Clean Air Act

2. _________ is individual power based on a high level of identification with, admiration of, or respect for the powerholder.

Nationalism, Patriotism, Celebrities and well-respected people are examples of _________ in effect.

_________ is one of the Five Bases of Social Power, as defined by Bertram Raven and his colleagues[1] in 1959.

a. 28-hour day
b. 1990 Clean Air Act
c. 33 Strategies of War
d. Referent power

3. _________ is a trait taught by many personal development experts and psychotherapists and the subject of many popular self-help books. It is linked to self-esteem and considered an important communication skill.

As a communication style and strategy, _________ is distinguished from aggression and passivity.

a. Intrinsic motivation
b. Assertiveness
c. A4e
d. A Stake in the Outcome

4.

_________ is a commonly used, yet poorly defined concept in industrial and organizational psychology, the branch of psychology that deals with the workplace. It most commonly refers to whether a person performs their job well. Despite the confusion over how it should be exactly defined, performance is an extremely important criterion that relates to organizational outcomes and success.

a. 28-hour day
b. Job performance
c. 1990 Clean Air Act
d. 33 Strategies of War

5. The _________ refers to situations in which students perform better than other students simply because they are expected to do so. The effect is named after George Bernard Shaw's play Pygmalion, in which a professor makes a bet that he can teach a poor flower girl to speak and act like an upper-class lady, and is successful.

The _________ requires a student to internalize the expectations of their superiors.

a. Distinction bias
b. Confirmation bias
c. Halo effect
d. Pygmalion effect

6. A _________ is an alliance among individuals or groups, during which they cooperate in joint action, each in his own self-interest, joining forces together for a common cause. This alliance may be temporary or a matter of convenience. A _________ thus differs from a more formal covenant.

a. 33 Strategies of War
b. 28-hour day
c. Coalition
d. 1990 Clean Air Act

7. _________ refers to increasing the spiritual, political, social or economic strength of individuals and communities. It often involves the empowered developing confidence in their own capacities.

The term Human _________ covers a vast landscape of meanings, interpretations, definitions and disciplines ranging from psychology and philosophy to the highly commercialized Self-Help industry and Motivational sciences.

a. AAAI
b. A Stake in the Outcome
c. A4e
d. Empowerment

8. _________ and Theory Y are theories of human motivation created and developed by Douglas McGregor at the MIT Sloan School of Management in the 1960s that have been used in human resource management, organizational behavior, organizational communication and organizational development. They describe two very different attitudes toward workforce motivation. McGregor felt that companies followed either one or the other approach.

In _________, which many managers practice, management assumes employees are inherently lazy and will avoid work if they can. They inherently dislike work. Because of this, workers need to be closely supervised and comprehensive systems of controls developed.

a. Cash cow
b. Theory X
c. Management team
d. Job enrichment

9. Theory X and _________ are theories of human motivation created and developed by Douglas McGregor at the MIT Sloan School of Management in the 1960s that have been used in human resource management, organizational behavior, organizational communication and organizational development. They describe two very different attitudes toward workforce motivation. McGregor felt that companies followed either one or the other approach.

In _________, management assumes employees may be ambitious and self-motivated and exercise self-control. It is believed that employees enjoy their mental and physical work duties.

a. Theory Y
b. Business Workflow Analysis
c. Design leadership
d. Contingency theory

10. _________ is a worldwide management consulting firm that focuses on solving issues of concern to senior management. McKinsey serves as an advisor to the world's leading businesses, governments, and institutions. It is widely recognized as a leader and one of the most prestigious firms in the management consulting industry.
a. 28-hour day
b. 1990 Clean Air Act
c. McKinsey ' Company
d. 33 Strategies of War

11. _________, widely known as F. W. Taylor, was an American mechanical engineer who sought to improve industrial efficiency. He is regarded as the father of scientific management, and was one of the first management consultants.

Taylor was one of the intellectual leaders of the Efficiency Movement and his ideas, broadly conceived, were highly influential in the Progressive Era.

a. Geoffrey Colvin
b. Jonah Jacob Goldberg
c. Douglas N. Daft
d. Frederick Winslow Taylor

12. _________ is a strategic planning method used to evaluate the Strengths, Weaknesses, Opportunities, and Threats involved in a project or in a business venture. It involves specifying the objective of the business venture or project and identifying the internal and external factors that are favorable and unfavorable to achieving that objective. The technique is credited to Albert Humphrey, who led a convention at Stanford University in the 1960s and 1970s using data from Fortune 500 companies.
a. Marketing
b. Market share
c. SWOT analysis
d. Corporate image

13. Contingency leadership theory in organizational studies is a type of leadership theory, leadership style, and leadership model that presumes that different leadership styles are contingent to different situations. It is also referred as _________Â® theory although, as originally convened, the situational theory term is much more restrictive. The original situational theory argues that the best type of leadership is totally determined by the situational variables.Currently there are many styles of leadership.
a. Situational theory
b. 28-hour day
c. Situational leadership
d. 1990 Clean Air Act

14. _________ , often measured as an _________ Quotient (EQ), is a term that describes the ability, capacity, skill or (in the case of the trait _________ model) a self-perceived ability, to identify, assess, and manage the emotions of one's self, of others, and of groups. Different models have been proposed for the definition of _________ and disagreement exists as to how the term should be used. Despite these disagreements, which are often highly technical, the ability _________ and trait _________ models (but not the mixed models) are enjoying considerable support in the literature and have successful applications in many different domains.
a. A4e
b. AAAI
c. Emotional intelligence
d. A Stake in the Outcome

15. The sociologist Max Weber defined _________ as 'resting on devotion to the exceptional sanctity, heroism or exemplary character of an individual person, and of the normative patterns or order revealed or ordained by him.' _________ is one of three forms of authority laid out in Weber's tripartite classification of authority, the other two being traditional authority and rational-legal authority. The concept has acquired wide usage among sociologists.

In his writings about _________, Weber applies the term charisma to 'a certain quality of an individual personality, by virtue of which he is set apart from ordinary men and treated as endowed with supernatural, superhuman, or at least specifically exceptional powers or qualities.

a. 1990 Clean Air Act
b. Rational-legal authority
c. 28-hour day
d. Charismatic authority

16. _________ is an advertisement in which a particular product specifically mentions a competitor by name for the express purpose of showing why the competitor is inferior to the product naming it.

This should not be confused with parody advertisements, where a fictional product is being advertised for the purpose of poking fun at the particular advertisement, nor should it be confused with the use of a coined brand name for the purpose of comparing the product without actually naming an actual competitor. ('Wikipedia tastes better and is less filling than the Encyclopedia Galactica.')

In the 1980s, during what has been referred to as the cola wars, soft-drink manufacturer Pepsi ran a series of advertisements where people, caught on hidden camera, in a blind taste test, chose Pepsi over rival Coca-Cola.

a. Comparative advertising
b. 28-hour day
c. 1990 Clean Air Act
d. 33 Strategies of War

1. _________ describes the relocation by a company of a business process from one country to another -- typically an operational process, such as manufacturing such as accounting. Even state governments employ _________.

The term is in use in several distinct but closely related ways.

a. A Stake in the Outcome
b. AAAI
c. A4e
d. Offshoring

2. _________ (NYSE: DE) is an American corporation based in Moline, Illinois, and the leading manufacturer of agricultural machinery in the world. In 2008, it was listed as 102nd in the Fortune 500 ranking. Deere and Company agricultural products, usually sold under the John Deere name, include tractors, combine harvesters, balers, planters/seeders, ATVs and forestry equipment.
a. 33 Strategies of War
b. 28-hour day
c. Deere ' Company
d. 1990 Clean Air Act

3. _________ is subcontracting a process, such as product design or manufacturing, to a third-party company. The decision to outsource is often made in the interest of lowering cost or making better use of time and energy costs, redirecting or conserving energy directed at the competencies of a particular business, or to make more efficient use of land, labor, capital, (information) technology and resources. _________ became part of the business lexicon during the 1980s.
a. Operant conditioning
b. Opinion leadership
c. Outsourcing
d. Unemployment insurance

4. The _________ 1970 is an Act of the United Kingdom Parliament which prohibits any less favourable treatment between men and women in terms of pay and conditions of employment. It came into force on 29 December 1975. The term pay is interpreted in a broad sense to include, on top of wages, things like holidays, pension rights, company perks and some kinds of bonuses.
a. Oncale v. Sundowner Offshore Services
b. Architectural Barriers Act of 1968
c. Australian labour law
d. Equal Pay Act

5. _________ is a term that has been used in various psychology theories, often in slightly different ways (e.g., Goldstein, Maslow, Rogers.) The term was originally introduced by the organismic theorist Kurt Goldstein for the motive to realise all of one's potentialities. In his view, it is the master motive--indeed, the only real motive a person has, all others being merely manifestations of it.

a. 28-hour day
b. 33 Strategies of War
c. 1990 Clean Air Act
d. Self-actualization

6. The _________ refers to situations in which students perform better than other students simply because they are expected to do so. The effect is named after George Bernard Shaw's play Pygmalion, in which a professor makes a bet that he can teach a poor flower girl to speak and act like an upper-class lady, and is successful.

The _________ requires a student to internalize the expectations of their superiors.

a. Confirmation bias
b. Halo effect
c. Distinction bias
d. Pygmalion effect

7. In law, _________ is the term to describe a partnership between two or more parties.

In England a number of statutes on the subject have been passed, the chief being the Bastardy Act of 1845, and the Bastardy Laws Amendment Acts of 1872 and 1873. The mother of a bastard may summon the putative father to petty sessions within twelve months of the birth (or at any later time if he is proved to have contributed to the child's support within twelve months after the birth), and the justices, as after hearing evidence on both sides, may, if the mother's evidence be corroborated in some material particular, adjudge the man to be the putative father of the child, and order him to pay a sum not exceeding five shillings a week for its maintenance, together with a sum for expenses incidental to the birth, or the funeral expenses, if it has died before the date of order, and the costs of the proceedings.

a. Abraham Harold Maslow
b. Affiliation
c. Adam Smith
d. Affiliation

8. Procter is a surname, and may also refer to:

- Bryan Waller Procter (pseud. Barry Cornwall), English poet
- Goodwin Procter, American law firm
- _________, consumer products multinational

a. Downstream
b. Master and Servant Acts
c. Strict liability
d. Procter ' Gamble

9. In psychology, _________ reflects a person's overall evaluation or appraisal of his or her own worth.

_________ encompasses beliefs (for example, 'I am competent/incompetent') and emotions (for example, triumph/despair, pride/shame.) Behavior may reflect _________

a. Self-esteem
b. 1990 Clean Air Act
c. 33 Strategies of War
d. 28-hour day

10. In decision theory and estimation theory, the _________ of an estimator, $\hat{\theta}$, of an unknown parameter of the distribution, θ, is the expected value of the loss function

$$R(\theta, \hat{\theta}) = \mathbb{E}_\theta L(\theta, \hat{\theta}) = \int L(\theta, \hat{\theta})\, dP_\theta.$$

where dP_θ is a probability measure parametrized by θ.

- For a scalar parameter θ and a quadratic loss function,

  $$L(\theta, \hat{\theta}) = (\theta - \hat{\theta})^2$$

  the _________ function becomes the mean squared error of the estimate,

  $$R(\theta, \hat{\theta}) = E_\theta(\theta - \hat{\theta})^2$$

- In density estimation, the unknown parameter is probability density itself. The loss function is typically chosen to be a norm in an appropriate function space. For example, for L^2 norm,

  $$L(f, \hat{f}) = \|f - \hat{f}\|_2^2$$

  the _________ function becomes the mean integrated squared error

  $$R(f, \hat{f}) = E\|f - \hat{f}\|^2$$

.

a. Linear model
b. Risk aversion
c. Financial modeling
d. Risk

11. The _________ of 2002 (Pub.L. 107-204, 116 Stat. 745, enacted July 30, 2002), also known as the Public Company Accounting Reform and Investor Protection Act of 2002 and commonly called Sarbanes-Oxley, Sarbox or SOX, is a United States federal law enacted on July 30, 2002, as a reaction to a number of major corporate and accounting scandals including those affecting Enron, Tyco International, Adelphia, Peregrine Systems and WorldCom.
a. Sarbanes-Oxley Act of 2002
b. Letter of credit
c. Fair Labor Standards Act
d. Sarbanes-Oxley Act

12. _________ was developed by Frederick Herzberg, a psychologist who found that job satisfaction and job dissatisfaction acted independently of each other. _________ states that there are certain factors in the workplace that cause job satisfaction, while a separate set of factors cause dissatisfaction.

a. 1990 Clean Air Act
b. Need for Achievement
c. Need for power
d. Two-factor theory

13. _________ involves establishing specific, measurable and time-targeted objectives. Work on the theory of goal-setting suggests that it's an effective tool for making progress by ensuring that participants in a group with a common goal are clearly aware of what is expected from them if an objective is to be achieved. On a personal level, setting goals is a process that allows people to specify then work towards their own objectives - most commonly with financial or career-based goals.
a. Digital strategy
b. Goal setting
c. Resource-based view
d. Catfish effect

14. _________ is the use of empirically demonstrated behavior change techniques to improve behavior, such as altering an individual's behaviors and reactions to stimuli through positive and negative reinforcement of adaptive behavior and/or the reduction of maladaptive behavior through punishment and/or therapy.

The first use of the term _________ appears to have been by Edward Thorndike in 1911

a. 1990 Clean Air Act
b. 28-hour day
c. Behavior modification
d. 33 Strategies of War

15. In operant conditioning, _________ occurs when an event following a response causes an increase in the probability of that response occurring in the future. Response strength can be assessed by measures such as the frequency with which the response is made (for example, a pigeon may peck a key more times in the session), or the speed with which it is made (for example, a rat may run a maze faster.) The environment change contingent upon the response is called a reinforcer.
a. Diminishing Manufacturing Sources and Material Shortages
b. Meetings, Incentives, Conferences, and Exhibitions
c. Historiometry
d. Reinforcement

16. _________ is about the mental processes regarding choice, or choosing. It explains the processes that an individual undergoes to make choices. In organizational behavior study, _________ is a motivation theory first proposed by Victor Vroom of the Yale School of Management.

a. A Stake in the Outcome
b. Expectancy theory
c. A4e
d. AAAI

17. In economics and sociology, an _________ is any factor (financial or non-financial) that enables or motivates a particular course of action, or counts as a reason for preferring one choice to the alternatives. It is an expectation that encourages people to behave in a certain way. Since human beings are purposeful creatures, the study of _________ structures is central to the study of all economic activity (both in terms of individual decision-making and in terms of co-operation and competition within a larger institutional structure.)
a. Incentive
b. AAAI
c. A4e
d. A Stake in the Outcome

18. _________ is a term describing performance-related pay, most frequently in the context of educational reform. It provides bonuses for workers who perform their jobs better, according to measurable criteria. In the United States, policy makers are divided on whether _________ should be offered to public school teachers, as is commonly the case in the United Kingdom.
a. Merit pay
b. Performance-related pay
c. Real wage
d. Profit-sharing agreement

19. _________ is the state or fact of exclusive rights and control over property, which may be an object, land/real estate or intellectual property. An _________ right is also referred to as title. The concept of _________ has existed for thousands of years and in all cultures.
a. A4e
b. A Stake in the Outcome
c. Emanation of the state
d. Ownership

20. In finance, an _________ is a contract between a buyer and a seller that gives the buyer the right--but not the obligation--to buy or to sell a particular asset (the underlying asset) at a later day at an agreed price. In return for granting the _________, the seller collects a payment (the premium) from the buyer. A call _________ gives the buyer the right to buy the underlying asset; a put _________ gives the buyer of the _________ the right to sell the underlying asset.

a. AAAI
b. A4e
c. A Stake in the Outcome
d. Option

1. _________ describes the situation when output from (or information about the result of) an event or phenomenon in the past will influence the same event/phenomenon in the present or future. When an event is part of a chain of cause-and-effect that forms a circuit or loop, then the event is said to 'feed back' into itself.

_________ is also a synonym for:

- _________ signal; the information about the initial event that is the basis for subsequent modification of the event.
- _________ loop; the causal path that leads from the initial generation of the _________ signal to the subsequent modification of the event.

_________ is a mechanism, process or signal that is looped back to control a system within itself. Such a loop is called a _________ loop.

a. Feedback loop
b. Feedback
c. Positive feedback
d. 1990 Clean Air Act

2. The _________ is a decision making method for use among groups of many sizes, who want to make their decision quickly, as by a vote, but want everyone's opinions taken into account (as opposed to traditional voting, where only the largest group is considered) . The method of tallying is the difference. First, every member of the group gives their view of the solution, with a short explanation.

a. Decision model
b. Belief decision matrix
c. Hierarchical Decision Process
d. Nominal group technique

3.

_________ is a commonly used, yet poorly defined concept in industrial and organizational psychology, the branch of psychology that deals with the workplace. It most commonly refers to whether a person performs their job well. Despite the confusion over how it should be exactly defined, performance is an extremely important criterion that relates to organizational outcomes and success.

a. 28-hour day
b. 33 Strategies of War
c. 1990 Clean Air Act
d. Job performance

4. _________ is a way of expressing knowledge or belief that an event will occur or has occurred. In mathematics the concept has been given an exact meaning in _________ theory, that is used extensively in such areas of study as mathematics, statistics, finance, gambling, science, and philosophy to draw conclusions about the likelihood of potential events and the underlying mechanics of complex systems.

The word _________ does not have a consistent direct definition.

a. Probability
b. Statistics
c. Time series analysis
d. Standard deviation

5. _________ is an advertisement in which a particular product specifically mentions a competitor by name for the express purpose of showing why the competitor is inferior to the product naming it.

This should not be confused with parody advertisements, where a fictional product is being advertised for the purpose of poking fun at the particular advertisement, nor should it be confused with the use of a coined brand name for the purpose of comparing the product without actually naming an actual competitor. ('Wikipedia tastes better and is less filling than the Encyclopedia Galactica.')

In the 1980s, during what has been referred to as the cola wars, soft-drink manufacturer Pepsi ran a series of advertisements where people, caught on hidden camera, in a blind taste test, chose Pepsi over rival Coca-Cola.

a. 1990 Clean Air Act
b. 28-hour day
c. 33 Strategies of War
d. Comparative advertising

6. _________ is an organization's process of defining its strategy and making decisions on allocating its resources to pursue this strategy, including its capital and people. Various business analysis techniques can be used in _________, including SWOT analysis (Strengths, Weaknesses, Opportunities, and Threats) and PEST analysis (Political, Economic, Social, and Technological analysis) or STEER analysis involving Socio-cultural, Technological, Economic, Ecological, and Regulatory factors and EPISTEL (Environment, Political, Informatic, Social, Technological, Economic and Legal)

_________ is the formal consideration of an organization's future course. All _________ deals with at least one of three key questions:

1. 'What do we do?'
2. 'For whom do we do it?'
3. 'How do we excel?'

In business _________, the third question is better phrased 'How can we beat or avoid competition?'. (Bradford and Duncan, page 1.)

a. 1990 Clean Air Act
b. 28-hour day
c. 33 Strategies of War
d. Strategic planning

7. A _________ is typically described as a deliberate plan of action to guide decisions and achieve rational outcome(s.) However, the term may also be used to denote what is actually done, even though it is unplanned.

The term may apply to government, private sector organizations and groups, and individuals.

a. Policy
b. 33 Strategies of War
c. 1990 Clean Air Act
d. 28-hour day

8. _________ is an area of knowledge within organizational theory that studies models and theories about the way an organization learns and adapts.

In Organizational development (OD), learning is a characteristic of an adaptive organization, i.e., an organization that is able to sense changes in signals from its environment (both internal and external) and adapt accordingly.

a. Organizational learning
b. A4e
c. A Stake in the Outcome
d. AAAI

9. A _________ is an organizational leader, responsible for ensuring that the organization maximizes the value it achieves through 'knowledge'. The _________ is responsible for managing intellectual capital and the custodian of Knowledge Management practices in an organization. _________ is not just a relabelling of the title 'chief information officer' - the _________ role is much broader.

a. Managing director
b. Chief knowledge officer
c. Hotel manager
d. General Manager

10. _________ comprises a range of practices used in an organisation to identify, create, represent, distribute and enable adoption of insights and experiences. Such insights and experiences comprise knowledge, either embodied in individuals or embedded in organisational processes or practice.

An established discipline since 1991 , _________ includes courses taught in the fields of business administration, information systems, management, and library and information sciences .

a. 33 Strategies of War
b. 28-hour day
c. Knowledge management
d. 1990 Clean Air Act

11. _________ (NYSE: DE) is an American corporation based in Moline, Illinois, and the leading manufacturer of agricultural machinery in the world. In 2008, it was listed as 102nd in the Fortune 500 ranking. Deere and Company agricultural products, usually sold under the John Deere name, include tractors, combine harvesters, balers, planters/seeders, ATVs and forestry equipment.

a. 1990 Clean Air Act
b. Deere ' Company
c. 33 Strategies of War
d. 28-hour day

12. The _________ refers to situations in which students perform better than other students simply because they are expected to do so. The effect is named after George Bernard Shaw's play Pygmalion, in which a professor makes a bet that he can teach a poor flower girl to speak and act like an upper-class lady, and is successful.

The _________ requires a student to internalize the expectations of their superiors.

a. Halo effect
b. Distinction bias
c. Confirmation bias
d. Pygmalion effect

13. _________ is a trait taught by many personal development experts and psychotherapists and the subject of many popular self-help books. It is linked to self-esteem and considered an important communication skill.

As a communication style and strategy, _________ is distinguished from aggression and passivity.

a. A4e
b. A Stake in the Outcome
c. Intrinsic motivation
d. Assertiveness

14. _________ in Public Relations

There are different types of _________ in public relations; symmetric and asymmetric.

Two-way asymmetric public relations...>· can also be called 'scientific persuasion;'>· employs social science methods to develop more persuasive communication;>· generally focuses on achieving short-term attitude change;>· incorporates lots of feedback from target audiences and publics;>· is used by an organization primarily interested in having its publics come around to its way of thinking rather changing the organization, its policies, or its views.

Two-way symmetric public relations...>· relies on honest and open _________ and mutual give-and-take rather than one-way persuasion;>· focuses on mutual respect and efforts to achieve mutual understanding;>· emphasizes negotiation and a willingness to adapt and make compromises;>· requires organizations engaging in public relations to be willing to make significant adjustments in how they operate in order to accommodate their publics;>· seems to be used more by non-profit organizations, government agencies, and heavily regulated businesses such as public utilities than by competitive, profit-driven companies.

a. 1990 Clean Air Act
b. 28-hour day
c. Two-way communication
d. Public relations

15. _________, widely known as F. W. Taylor, was an American mechanical engineer who sought to improve industrial efficiency. He is regarded as the father of scientific management, and was one of the first management consultants.

Taylor was one of the intellectual leaders of the Efficiency Movement and his ideas, broadly conceived, were highly influential in the Progressive Era.

a. Frederick Winslow Taylor
b. Jonah Jacob Goldberg
c. Geoffrey Colvin
d. Douglas N. Daft

1. _________, widely known as F. W. Taylor, was an American mechanical engineer who sought to improve industrial efficiency. He is regarded as the father of scientific management, and was one of the first management consultants.

Taylor was one of the intellectual leaders of the Efficiency Movement and his ideas, broadly conceived, were highly influential in the Progressive Era.

a. Douglas N. Daft
b. Geoffrey Colvin
c. Jonah Jacob Goldberg
d. Frederick Winslow Taylor

2.

_________ is a commonly used, yet poorly defined concept in industrial and organizational psychology, the branch of psychology that deals with the workplace. It most commonly refers to whether a person performs their job well. Despite the confusion over how it should be exactly defined, performance is an extremely important criterion that relates to organizational outcomes and success.

a. 1990 Clean Air Act
b. 33 Strategies of War
c. 28-hour day
d. Job performance

3. In mathematics, a _________ law is (roughly speaking) a formal power series behaving as if it were the product of a Lie group. They were first defined in 1946 by S. Bochner. The term _________ sometimes means the same as _________ law, and sometimes means one of several generalizations.

a. 33 Strategies of War
b. 28-hour day
c. Formal group
d. 1990 Clean Air Act

4. Procter is a surname, and may also refer to:

- Bryan Waller Procter (pseud. Barry Cornwall), English poet
- Goodwin Procter, American law firm
- _________, consumer products multinational

a. Downstream
b. Master and Servant Acts
c. Strict liability
d. Procter ' Gamble

5. _________ refers to the movement of cash into or out of a business or financial product. It is usually measured during a specified, finite period of time. Measurement of _________ can be used

- to determine a project's rate of return or value. The time of _________s into and out of projects are used as inputs in financial models such as internal rate of return, and net present value.
- to determine problems with a business's liquidity. Being profitable does not necessarily mean being liquid. A company can fall because of a shortage of cash, even while profitable.
- as an alternate measure of a business's profits when it is believed that accrual accounting concepts do not represent economic realities. For example, a company may be notionally profitable but generating little operational cash (as may be the case for a company that barters its products rather than selling for cash.) In such a case, the company may be deriving additional operating cash by issuing shares evaluating default risk, re-investment requirements, etc.

_________ is a generic term used differently depending on the context. It may be defined by users for their own purposes.

a. Cash flow
b. Sweat equity
c. Gross profit
d. Gross profit margin

6. A _________ is a group of employees from various functional areas of the organization - research, engineering, marketing, finance. human resources, and operations, for example - who are all focused on a specific objective and are responsible to work as a team to improve coordination and innovation across divisions and resolve mutual problems.
a. Graduate recruitment
b. Sociotechnical systems
c. Goal-setting theory
d. Cross-functional team

7. _________ is a group creativity technique designed to generate a large number of ideas for the solution of a problem. The method was first popularized in the late 1930s by Alex Faickney Osborn in a book called Applied Imagination. Osborn proposed that groups could double their creative output with _________.

a. Adam Smith
b. Abraham Harold Maslow
c. Affiliation
d. Brainstorming

8. A _________ -- also known as a geographically dispersed team -- is a group of individuals who work across time, space, and organizational boundaries with links strengthened by webs of communication technology. They have complementary skills and are committed to a common purpose, have interdependent performance goals, and share an approach to work for which they hold themselves mutually accountable. Geographically dispersed teams allow organizations to hire and retain the best people regardless of location.
a. Trademark
b. Kanban
c. Risk management
d. Virtual team

9. In organizational development (OD), _________ is the application of Socio-Technical Systems principles and techniques to the humanization of work.

The aims of _________ to improved job satisfaction, to improved through-put, to improved quality and to reduced employee problems, e.g., grievances, absenteeism.

Under scientific management people would be directed by reason and the problems of industrial unrest would be appropriately (i.e., scientifically) addressed.

a. Work design
b. Graduate recruitment
c. Management process
d. Path-goal theory

10. _________ is a dynamic of being mutually and physically responsible to and sharing a common set of principles with others. This concept differs distinctly from 'dependence' in that an interdependent relationship implies that all participants are emotionally, economically, ecologically and or morally 'interdependent.' Some people advocate freedom or independence as a sort of ultimate good; others do the same with devotion to one's family, community, or society. _________ recognizes the truth in each position and weaves them together.
a. A Stake in the Outcome
b. Interdependence
c. AAAI
d. A4e

11. _________ , often measured as an _________ Quotient (EQ), is a term that describes the ability, capacity, skill or (in the case of the trait _________ model) a self-perceived ability, to identify, assess, and manage the emotions of one's self, of others, and of groups. Different models have been proposed for the definition of _________ and disagreement exists as to how the term should be used. Despite these disagreements, which are often highly technical, the ability _________ and trait _________ models (but not the mixed models) are enjoying considerable support in the literature and have successful applications in many different domains.

a. A4e
b. Emotional intelligence
c. AAAI
d. A Stake in the Outcome

12. The _________ is a decision making method for use among groups of many sizes, who want to make their decision quickly, as by a vote, but want everyone's opinions taken into account (as opposed to traditional voting, where only the largest group is considered) . The method of tallying is the difference. First, every member of the group gives their view of the solution, with a short explanation.

a. Nominal group technique
b. Hierarchical Decision Process
c. Decision model
d. Belief decision matrix

13. In business management, _________ is a management style where a manager closely observes or controls the work of his or her subordinates or employees. _________ is generally used as a negative term .

Webster's Dictionary defines micromanage as: 'to manage with great or excessive control, or attention to details'.

a. Getting Things Done
b. Decentralization
c. Management team
d. Micromanagement

14. The _________ refers to situations in which students perform better than other students simply because they are expected to do so. The effect is named after George Bernard Shaw's play Pygmalion, in which a professor makes a bet that he can teach a poor flower girl to speak and act like an upper-class lady, and is successful.

The _________ requires a student to internalize the expectations of their superiors.

a. Pygmalion effect
b. Halo effect
c. Distinction bias
d. Confirmation bias

15. _________ is a concept in ethics with several meanings. It is often used synonymously with such concepts as responsibility, answerability, enforcement, blameworthiness, liability and other terms associated with the expectation of account-giving. As an aspect of governance, it has been central to discussions related to problems in both the public and private (corporation) worlds.

a. A4e
b. Usury
c. A Stake in the Outcome
d. Accountability

16. In the social psychology of groups, _________ is the phenomenon of people making less effort to achieve a goal when they work in a group than when they work alone. This is seen as one of the main reasons groups are sometimes less productive than the combined performance of their members working as individuals.

- Ringelmann, Max : 1913

Research began in 1913 with Max Ringelmann's study. He found that when he asked a group of men to pull on a rope, that they did not pull as hard, or put as much effort into the activity, as they did when they were pulling alone.

a. Social loafing
b. Machiavellianism
c. Personal space
d. Self-enhancement

17. The phrase mergers and _________s refers to the aspect of corporate strategy, corporate finance and management dealing with the buying, selling and combining of different companies that can aid, finance, or help a growing company in a given industry grow rapidly without having to create another business entity.

An _________, also known as a takeover or a buyout, is the buying of one company (the 'target') by another. An _________ may be friendly or hostile.

a. Acquisition
b. A4e
c. A Stake in the Outcome
d. AAAI

18. _________ is a term defined by the Oxford English Dictionary as an individual's 'course or progress through life '. It is usually considered to pertain to remunerative work (and sometimes also formal education.)

The etymology of the term is somewhat ironic in that it comes from the Latin word carrera, which means race .

a. Career
b. Spatial mismatch
c. Nursing shortage
d. Career planning

19. _________ is a range of processes aimed at alleviating or eliminating sources of conflict. The term '_________' is sometimes used interchangeably with the term dispute resolution or alternative dispute resolution. Processes of _________ generally include negotiation, mediation and diplomacy.

a. 33 Strategies of War
b. Conflict resolution
c. 1990 Clean Air Act
d. 28-hour day

20. _________ is a strategic planning method used to evaluate the Strengths, Weaknesses, Opportunities, and Threats involved in a project or in a business venture. It involves specifying the objective of the business venture or project and identifying the internal and external factors that are favorable and unfavorable to achieving that objective. The technique is credited to Albert Humphrey, who led a convention at Stanford University in the 1960s and 1970s using data from Fortune 500 companies.

a. Corporate image
b. Market share
c. Marketing
d. SWOT analysis

21. _________ is a recursive process where two or more people or organizations work together in an intersection of common goals -- for example, an intellectual endeavor that is creative in nature--by sharing knowledge, learning and building consensus. _________ does not require leadership and can sometimes bring better results through decentralization and egalitarianism. In particular, teams that work collaboratively can obtain greater resources, recognition and reward when facing competition for finite resources._________ is also present in opposing goals exhibiting the notion of adversarial _________, though this is not a common case for using the term.

a. 28-hour day
b. 1990 Clean Air Act
c. Collectivism
d. Collaboration

22. _________ is a civil designation for persons who are incorporated in a fixed or permanent way to a society or group: regular member of the working staff, permanent staff distinguished from a supernumerary.

The term '_________' and its counterpart, 'supernumerary,' originated in Spanish and Latin American academy and government; it is now also used in countries all over the world, such as France, the U.S., England, Italy, etc.

There are _________ members of surgical organizations, of universities, of gastronomical associations, etc.

a. Numerary
b. Affiliation
c. Abraham Harold Maslow
d. Adam Smith

23. _________ is one of the managerial functions like planning, organizing, staffing and directing. It is an important function because it helps to check the errors and to take the corrective action so that deviation from standards are minimized and stated goals of the organization are achieved in desired manner.According to modern concepts, _________ is a foreseeing action whereas earlier concept of _________ was used only when errors were detected. _________ in management means setting standards, measuring actual performance and taking corrective action.

a. Schedule of reinforcement
b. Decision tree pruning
c. Control
d. Turnover

1. Procter is a surname, and may also refer to:

- Bryan Waller Procter (pseud. Barry Cornwall), English poet
- Goodwin Procter, American law firm
- _________, consumer products multinational

.

a. Downstream
b. Master and Servant Acts
c. Strict liability
d. Procter ' Gamble

2. _________, widely known as F. W. Taylor, was an American mechanical engineer who sought to improve industrial efficiency. He is regarded as the father of scientific management, and was one of the first management consultants.

Taylor was one of the intellectual leaders of the Efficiency Movement and his ideas, broadly conceived, were highly influential in the Progressive Era.

a. Jonah Jacob Goldberg
b. Frederick Winslow Taylor
c. Geoffrey Colvin
d. Douglas N. Daft

3.

_________ is a commonly used, yet poorly defined concept in industrial and organizational psychology, the branch of psychology that deals with the workplace. It most commonly refers to whether a person performs their job well. Despite the confusion over how it should be exactly defined, performance is an extremely important criterion that relates to organizational outcomes and success.

a. 1990 Clean Air Act
b. 28-hour day
c. 33 Strategies of War
d. Job performance

4. A _________ is a framework for creating economic, social, and/or other forms of value. The term _________ is thus used for a broad range of informal and formal descriptions to represent core aspects of a business, including purpose, offerings, strategies, infrastructure, organizational structures, trading practices, and operational processes and policies.

Conceptualizations of _________s try to formalize informal descriptions into building blocks and their relationships.

a. Business model design
b. Business networking
c. Business model
d. Gap analysis

5. _________ of the learning curve effect and the closely related experience curve effect express the relationship between equations for experience and efficiency or between efficiency gains and investment in the effort. The experience of 'learning curves' was first observed by the 19th Century German psychologist Hermann Ebbinghaus according to the difficulty of memorizing varying numbers of verbal stimuli, and subsequent learning about the complex processes of learning are discussed in the

.

The rule used for representing the learning curve effect states that the more times a task has been performed, the less time will be required on each subsequent iteration.

a. Models
b. Point biserial correlation coefficient
c. Spatial Decision Support Systems
d. Distribution

6. An _________ is a private network that uses Internet protocols, network connectivity, and possibly the public telecommunication system to securely share part of an organization's information or operations with suppliers, vendors, partners, customers or other businesses. An _________ can be viewed as part of a company's intranet that is extended to users outside the company (e.g.: normally over the Internet.) It has also been described as a 'state of mind' in which the Internet is perceived as a way to do business with a preapproved set of other companies business-to-business (B2B), in isolation from all other Internet users.

a. A4e
b. AAAI
c. A Stake in the Outcome
d. Extranet

7. _________ is the provision of service to customers before, during and after a purchase.

According to Turban et al. (2002), '_________ is a series of activities designed to enhance the level of customer satisfaction - that is, the feeling that a product or service has met the customer expectation.'

Its importance varies by product, industry and customer; defective or broken merchandise can be exchanged, often only with a receipt and within a specified time frame.

a. Customer service
b. 1990 Clean Air Act
c. 28-hour day
d. Service rate

8. An _________ is a private computer network that uses Internet technologies to securely share any part of an organization's information or operational systems with its employees. Sometimes the term refers only to the organization's internal website, but often it is a more extensive part of the organization's computer infrastructure and private websites are an important component and focal point of internal communication and collaboration.

An _________ is built from the same concepts and technologies used for the Internet, such as client-server computing and the Internet Protocol Suite (TCP/IP.)

a. A Stake in the Outcome
b. AAAI
c. Intranet
d. A4e

9. _________ is an advertisement in which a particular product specifically mentions a competitor by name for the express purpose of showing why the competitor is inferior to the product naming it.

This should not be confused with parody advertisements, where a fictional product is being advertised for the purpose of poking fun at the particular advertisement, nor should it be confused with the use of a coined brand name for the purpose of comparing the product without actually naming an actual competitor. ('Wikipedia tastes better and is less filling than the Encyclopedia Galactica.')

In the 1980s, during what has been referred to as the cola wars, soft-drink manufacturer Pepsi ran a series of advertisements where people, caught on hidden camera, in a blind taste test, chose Pepsi over rival Coca-Cola.

a. 28-hour day
b. 33 Strategies of War
c. 1990 Clean Air Act
d. Comparative advertising

10. _________, commonly known as e-commerce, consists of the buying and selling of products or services over electronic systems such as the Internet and other computer networks. The amount of trade conducted electronically has grown extraordinarily with widespread Internet usage. The use of commerce is conducted in this way, spurring and drawing on innovations in electronic funds transfer, supply chain management, Internet marketing, online transaction processing, electronic data interchange (EDI), inventory management systems, and automated data collection systems.

a. A Stake in the Outcome
b. A4e
c. Online shopping
d. Electronic Commerce

11. _________ is one of the managerial functions like planning, organizing, staffing and directing. It is an important function because it helps to check the errors and to take the corrective action so that deviation from standards are minimized and stated goals of the organization are achieved in desired manner.According to modern concepts, _________ is a foreseeing action whereas earlier concept of _________ was used only when errors were detected. _________ in management means setting standards, measuring actual performance and taking corrective action.

a. Turnover
b. Schedule of reinforcement
c. Decision tree pruning
d. Control

12. In economics, business, retail, and accounting, a _________ is the value of money that has been used up to produce something, and hence is not available for use anymore. In economics, a _________ is an alternative that is given up as a result of a decision. In business, the _________ may be one of acquisition, in which case the amount of money expended to acquire it is counted as _________.

a. Cost allocation
b. Fixed costs
c. Cost
d. Cost overrun

13. _________ is the process whereby companies use cost accounting to report or control the various costs of doing business.

_________ generally describes the approaches and activities of managers in short run and long run planning and control decisions that increase value for customers and lower costs of products and services.

a. Cost Management
b. Genbutsu
c. Missing completely at random
d. Strict liability

14. _________ is, in very basic words, a position a firm occupies against its competitors.

According to Michael Porter, the three methods for creating a sustainable _________ are through:

1. Cost leadership

2. Differentiation

3. Focus (economics)

a. 1990 Clean Air Act
b. Theory Z
c. 28-hour day
d. Competitive advantage

15. _________ is the process of extracting hidden patterns from data. As more data is gathered, with the amount of data doubling every three years, _________ is becoming an increasingly important tool to transform this data into information. It is commonly used in a wide range of profiling practices, such as marketing, surveillance, fraud detection and scientific discovery.
a. Decision tree learning
b. 1990 Clean Air Act
c. Data mining
d. 28-hour day

1. _________ is one of the managerial functions like planning, organizing, staffing and directing. It is an important function because it helps to check the errors and to take the corrective action so that deviation from standards are minimized and stated goals of the organization are achieved in desired manner.According to modern concepts, _________ is a foreseeing action whereas earlier concept of _________ was used only when errors were detected. _________ in management means setting standards, measuring actual performance and taking corrective action.

a. Turnover
b. Decision tree pruning
c. Schedule of reinforcement
d. Control

2. In economics, business, retail, and accounting, a _________ is the value of money that has been used up to produce something, and hence is not available for use anymore. In economics, a _________ is an alternative that is given up as a result of a decision. In business, the _________ may be one of acquisition, in which case the amount of money expended to acquire it is counted as _________.

a. Cost
b. Cost allocation
c. Cost overrun
d. Fixed costs

3. _________ is the process whereby companies use cost accounting to report or control the various costs of doing business.

_________ generally describes the approaches and activities of managers in short run and long run planning and control decisions that increase value for customers and lower costs of products and services.

a. Missing completely at random
b. Genbutsu
c. Strict liability
d. Cost Management

4. A _________ is a type of bar chart that illustrates a project schedule. _________s illustrate the start and finish dates of the terminal elements and summary elements of a project. Terminal elements and summary elements comprise the work breakdown structure of the project.

a. 33 Strategies of War
b. Gantt chart
c. 1990 Clean Air Act
d. 28-hour day

5. _________ describes the situation when output from (or information about the result of) an event or phenomenon in the past will influence the same event/phenomenon in the present or future. When an event is part of a chain of cause-and-effect that forms a circuit or loop, then the event is said to 'feed back' into itself.

_________ is also a synonym for:

- _________ signal; the information about the initial event that is the basis for subsequent modification of the event.
- _________ loop; the causal path that leads from the initial generation of the _________ signal to the subsequent modification of the event.

_________ is a mechanism, process or signal that is looped back to control a system within itself. Such a loop is called a _________ loop.

a. Feedback loop
b. Positive feedback
c. 1990 Clean Air Act
d. Feedback

6. In accounting and auditing, _________ is defined as a process effected by an organization's structure, work and authority flows, people and management information systems, designed to help the organization accomplish specific goals or objectives. It is a means by which an organization's resources are directed, monitored, and measured. It plays an important role in preventing and detecting fraud and protecting the organization's resources, both physical (e.g., machinery and property) and intangible (e.g., reputation or intellectual property such as trademarks.)
a. A Stake in the Outcome
b. Internal auditing
c. Audit committee
d. Internal control

7. The _________ refers to situations in which students perform better than other students simply because they are expected to do so. The effect is named after George Bernard Shaw's play Pygmalion, in which a professor makes a bet that he can teach a poor flower girl to speak and act like an upper-class lady, and is successful.

The _________ requires a student to internalize the expectations of their superiors.

a. Confirmation bias
b. Halo effect
c. Pygmalion effect
d. Distinction bias

8. A _________ is a change implemented to address a weakness identified in a management system. Normally _________s are implemented in response to a customer complaint, abnormal levels of internal nonconformity, nonconformities identified during an internal audit or adverse or unstable trends in product and process monitoring such as would be identified by SPC.

The process of determining a _________ requires identification of actions that can be taken to prevent or mitigate the weakness.

a. 28-hour day
b. Zero defects
c. Corrective action
d. 1990 Clean Air Act

9. The _________ is a decision making method for use among groups of many sizes, who want to make their decision quickly, as by a vote, but want everyone's opinions taken into account (as opposed to traditional voting, where only the largest group is considered) . The method of tallying is the difference. First, every member of the group gives their view of the solution, with a short explanation.
a. Belief decision matrix
b. Hierarchical Decision Process
c. Decision model
d. Nominal group technique

10. _________ generally refers to a list of all planned expenses and revenues. It is a plan for saving and spending. A _________ is an important concept in microeconomics, which uses a _________ line to illustrate the trade-offs between two or more goods.
a. Budget
b. 28-hour day
c. 33 Strategies of War
d. 1990 Clean Air Act

11. The _________ of 2002 (Pub.L. 107-204, 116 Stat. 745, enacted July 30, 2002), also known as the Public Company Accounting Reform and Investor Protection Act of 2002 and commonly called Sarbanes-Oxley, Sarbox or SOX, is a United States federal law enacted on July 30, 2002, as a reaction to a number of major corporate and accounting scandals including those affecting Enron, Tyco International, Adelphia, Peregrine Systems and WorldCom.
a. Sarbanes-Oxley Act of 2002
b. Letter of credit
c. Fair Labor Standards Act
d. Sarbanes-Oxley Act

12. The general definition of an _________ is an evaluation of a person, organization, system, process, project or product. _________s are performed to ascertain the validity and reliability of information; also to provide an assessment of a system's internal control. The goal of an _________ is to express an opinion on the person / organization/system (etc) in question, under evaluation based on work done on a test basis.

a. Internal control
b. Audit committee
c. A Stake in the Outcome
d. Audit

13. _________ is a medical condition in which the median nerve is compressed at the wrist, leading to paresthesias, numbness and muscle weakness in the hand. The diagnosis of _________ is often misapplied to patients who have activity-related arm pain.

Most cases of _________ are idiopathic (without known cause); genetic factors determine most of the risk, and the role of arm use and other environmental factors is disputed.

a. 28-hour day
b. 1990 Clean Air Act
c. 33 Strategies of War
d. Carpal tunnel syndrome

14. Procter is a surname, and may also refer to:

- Bryan Waller Procter (pseud. Barry Cornwall), English poet
- Goodwin Procter, American law firm
- _________, consumer products multinational

.

a. Procter ' Gamble
b. Master and Servant Acts
c. Downstream
d. Strict liability

15. _________s (CAPEX or capex) are expenditures creating future benefits. A _________ is incurred when a business spends money either to buy fixed assets or to add to the value of an existing fixed asset with a useful life that extends beyond the taxable year. Capex are used by a company to acquire or upgrade physical assets such as equipment, property, or industrial buildings.

a. Capital expenditure
b. Capital intensive
c. 1990 Clean Air Act
d. Weighted average cost of capital

16. _________ refers to the movement of cash into or out of a business or financial product. It is usually measured during a specified, finite period of time. Measurement of _________ can be used

- to determine a project's rate of return or value. The time of _________s into and out of projects are used as inputs in financial models such as internal rate of return, and net present value.
- to determine problems with a business's liquidity. Being profitable does not necessarily mean being liquid. A company can fail because of a shortage of cash, even while profitable.
- as an alternate measure of a business's profits when it is believed that accrual accounting concepts do not represent economic realities. For example, a company may be notionally profitable but generating little operational cash (as may be the case for a company that barters its products rather than selling for cash.) In such a case, the company may be deriving additional operating cash by issuing shares evaluating default risk, re-investment requirements, etc.

_________ is a generic term used differently depending on the context. It may be defined by users for their own purposes.

a. Sweat equity
b. Gross profit
c. Cash flow
d. Gross profit margin

17. In finance, a _________ or accounting ratio is a ratio of two selected numerical values taken from an enterprise's financial statements. There are many standard ratios used to try to evaluate the overall financial condition of a corporation or other organization. _________s may be used by managers within a firm, by current and potential shareholders (owners) of a firm, and by a firm's creditors.

a. Return on equity
b. Rate of return
c. Return on sales
d. Financial ratio

18. In accounting, _________ or sales profit is the difference between revenue and the cost of making a product or providing a service, before deducting overhead, payroll, taxation, and interest payments. Note that this is different from operating profit (earnings before interest and taxes.)

Net sales are calculated:

Net sales = Sales - Sales returns and allowances.

a. Capital budgeting
b. Cash flow
c. Gross profit margin
d. Gross profit

19. _________ is a financial ratio used to assess the profitability of a firm's core activities, excluding fixed costs.

The general calculation is:

>

The _________ is related to the net profit margin, which assesses the profitability of an organization after including fixed costs.

_________ indicates the relationship between net sales revenue and the cost of goods sold.

a. Capital structure
b. Shareholder value
c. Sweat equity
d. Gross profit margin

20. _________, net margin, net _________ or net profit ratio all refer to a measure of profitability. It is calculated by finding the net profit as a percentage of the revenue.

$$\text{Net profit margin} = \frac{\text{Net profit (after taxes)}}{\text{Revenue}} \times 100\%$$

The _________ is mostly used for internal comparison.

a. Profit margin
b. Net profit margin
c. 1990 Clean Air Act
d. Profit maximization

21. _________(requity)measures the rate of return on the ownership interest (shareholders' equity) of the common stock owners. It measures a firm's efficiency at generating profits from every dollar of shareholders' equity (also known as net assets or assets minus liabilities.) It shows how well a company uses investment dollars to generate earnings growth.

a. Financial ratio
b. Return on equity
c. Return on Capital Employed
d. Rate of return

22. The _________ is an expected return that the provider of capital plans to earn on their investment.

Capital (money) used for funding a business should earn returns for the capital providers who risk their capital. For an investment to be worthwhile, the expected return on capital must be greater than the _________.

a. Cost of capital
b. Capital intensive
c. Weighted average cost of capital
d. 1990 Clean Air Act

23. _________ is a term used in accounting, economics and finance to spread the cost of an asset over the span of several years.

In simple words we can say that _________ is the reduction in the value of an asset due to usage, passage of time, wear and tear, technological outdating or obsolescence, depletion, inadequacy, rot, rust, decay or other such factors.

In accounting, _________ is a term used to describe any method of attributing the historical or purchase cost of an asset across its useful life, roughly corresponding to normal wear and tear.

a. Matching principle
b. Net profit
c. Treasury stock
d. Depreciation

24. In corporate finance, _________ or _________ is an estimate of true economic profit after making corrective adjustments to GAAP accounting, including deducting the opportunity cost of equity capital. _________ can be measured as Net Operating Profit After Taxes(or NOPAT) less the money cost of capital. _________ is similar in nature to that of calculating another financial performance measure - Residual Income , however, there are a few complexities involved with coming up with the elements for calculating _________ over RI such as the myriad adjustments that might be made to NOPAT before it is suitable for the formula below.

a. A Stake in the Outcome
b. AAAI
c. A4e
d. Economic value added

25. _________ refers to the difference between the cost of materials purchased by a company plus the cost of the labor to assemble a product and the price at which the company sells the product. An example is the price of gasoline at the pump over the price of the oil in it. In national accounts used in macroeconomics, it refers to the contribution of the factors of production, i.e., land, labor, and capital goods, to raising the value of a product and corresponds to the incomes received by the owners of these factors.
a. Value added
b. Deregulation
c. Rehn-Meidner Model
d. Minimum wage

26. In corporate finance, _________ is cash flow available for distribution among all the securities holders of an organization. They include equity holders, debt holders, preferred stock holders, convertible security holders, and so on.

Note that the first three lines above are calculated for you on the standard Statement of Cash Flows.

a. Policies and procedures
b. Kaizen
c. Pre-determined overhead rate
d. Free cash flow

27. _________ is an integrated communications-based process through which individuals and communities discover that existing and newly-identified needs and wants may be satisfied by the products and services of others.

_________ is defined by the American _________ Association as the activity, set of institutions, and processes for creating, communicating, delivering, and exchanging offerings that have value for customers, clients, partners, and society at large. The term developed from the original meaning which referred literally to going to market, as in shopping, or going to a market to buy or sell goods or services.

a. Disruptive technology
b. Customer relationship management
c. Market development
d. Marketing

28. _________ is an advertisement in which a particular product specifically mentions a competitor by name for the express purpose of showing why the competitor is inferior to the product naming it.

This should not be confused with parody advertisements, where a fictional product is being advertised for the purpose of poking fun at the particular advertisement, nor should it be confused with the use of a coined brand name for the purpose of comparing the product without actually naming an actual competitor. ('Wikipedia tastes better and is less filling than the Encyclopedia Galactica.')

In the 1980s, during what has been referred to as the cola wars, soft-drink manufacturer Pepsi ran a series of advertisements where people, caught on hidden camera, in a blind taste test, chose Pepsi over rival Coca-Cola.

a. 28-hour day
b. Comparative advertising
c. 1990 Clean Air Act
d. 33 Strategies of War

29. _________ is a costing model that identifies activities in an organization and assigns the cost of each activity resource to all products and services according to the actual consumption by each: it assigns more indirect costs (overhead) into direct costs.

In this way an organization can establish the true cost of its individual products and services for the purposes of identifying and eliminating those which are unprofitable and lowering the prices of those which are overpriced.

In a business organization, the ABC methodology assigns an organization's resource costs through activities to the products and services provided to its customers.

a. Indirect costs
b. A Stake in the Outcome
c. Activity-based costing
d. A4e

30. The _________ is a performance management tool for measuring whether the smaller-scale operational activities of a company are aligned with its larger-scale objectives in terms of vision and strategy.

By focusing not only on financial outcomes but also on the operational, marketing and developmental inputs to these, the _________ helps provide a more comprehensive view of a business, which in turn helps organizations act in their best long-term interests. This tool is also being used to address business response to climate change and greenhouse gas emissions.

a. Management development
b. Middle management
c. Commercial management
d. Balanced scorecard

31. The term _________ collectively refers to all resources that determine the value and the competitiveness of an enterprise. As such, it includes as subsets the attributes that concur to building all financial statements as well as the balance sheet.
a. AAAI
b. Intellectual capital
c. A Stake in the Outcome
d. A4e

32.

_________ is a commonly used, yet poorly defined concept in industrial and organizational psychology, the branch of psychology that deals with the workplace. It most commonly refers to whether a person performs their job well. Despite the confusion over how it should be exactly defined, performance is an extremely important criterion that relates to organizational outcomes and success.

a. 1990 Clean Air Act
b. 33 Strategies of War
c. 28-hour day
d. Job performance

33. A _________ is a subset of the overall internal controls of a business covering the application of people, documents, technologies, and procedures by management accountants to solving business problems such as costing a product, service or a business-wide strategy. _________s are distinct from regular information systems in that they are used to analyze other information systems applied in operational activities in the organization. Academically, the term is commonly used to refer to the group of information management methods tied to the automation or support of human decision making, e.g. Decision Support Systems, Expert systems, and Executive information systems.
a. 28-hour day
b. 1990 Clean Air Act
c. Strategic information system
d. Management information system

1. _________ is one of the managerial functions like planning, organizing, staffing and directing. It is an important function because it helps to check the errors and to take the corrective action so that deviation from standards are minimized and stated goals of the organization are achieved in desired manner.According to modern concepts, _________ is a foreseeing action whereas earlier concept of _________ was used only when errors were detected. _________ in management means setting standards, measuring actual performance and taking corrective action.

a. Schedule of reinforcement
b. Turnover
c. Control
d. Decision tree pruning

2. In economics, business, retail, and accounting, a _________ is the value of money that has been used up to produce something, and hence is not available for use anymore. In economics, a _________ is an alternative that is given up as a result of a decision. In business, the _________ may be one of acquisition, in which case the amount of money expended to acquire it is counted as _________.

a. Cost
b. Cost allocation
c. Cost overrun
d. Fixed costs

3. _________ is the process whereby companies use cost accounting to report or control the various costs of doing business.

_________ generally describes the approaches and activities of managers in short run and long run planning and control decisions that increase value for customers and lower costs of products and services.

a. Genbutsu
b. Missing completely at random
c. Strict liability
d. Cost Management

4.

_________ is a commonly used, yet poorly defined concept in industrial and organizational psychology, the branch of psychology that deals with the workplace. It most commonly refers to whether a person performs their job well. Despite the confusion over how it should be exactly defined, performance is an extremely important criterion that relates to organizational outcomes and success.

a. 33 Strategies of War
b. 28-hour day
c. 1990 Clean Air Act
d. Job performance

5. The _________ of 1967, Pub. L. No. 90-202, 81 Stat. 602 (Dec. 15, 1967), codified as Chapter 14 of Title 29 of the United States Code, 29 U.S.C. Â§ 621 through 29 U.S.C. Â§ 634 (ADEA), prohibits employment discrimination against persons 40 years of age or older in the United States). The law also sets standards for pensions and benefits provided by employers and requires that information about the needs of older workers be provided to the general public.
a. Unemployment and Farm Relief Act
b. Age Discrimination in Employment Act
c. Undue hardship
d. Extra time

6. _________ is a contract between two parties, one being the employer and the other being the employee. An employee may be defined as: 'A person in the service of another under any contract of hire, express or implied, oral or written, where the employer has the power or right to control and direct the employee in the material details of how the work is to be performed.' Black's Law Dictionary page 471 (5th ed. 1979.)
a. Employment
b. Exit interview
c. Employment rate
d. Employment counsellor

7. _________ is a strategic planning method used to evaluate the Strengths, Weaknesses, Opportunities, and Threats involved in a project or in a business venture. It involves specifying the objective of the business venture or project and identifying the internal and external factors that are favorable and unfavorable to achieving that objective. The technique is credited to Albert Humphrey, who led a convention at Stanford University in the 1960s and 1970s using data from Fortune 500 companies.
a. Corporate image
b. Marketing
c. Market share
d. SWOT analysis

8. _________, widely known as F. W. Taylor, was an American mechanical engineer who sought to improve industrial efficiency. He is regarded as the father of scientific management, and was one of the first management consultants.

Taylor was one of the intellectual leaders of the Efficiency Movement and his ideas, broadly conceived, were highly influential in the Progressive Era.

a. Douglas N. Daft
b. Frederick Winslow Taylor
c. Jonah Jacob Goldberg
d. Geoffrey Colvin

9. _________ is a habitual pattern of absence from a duty or obligation.

Frequent absence from the workplace may be indicative of poor morale or of sick building syndrome. However, many employers have implemented absence policies which make no distinction between absences for genuine illness and absence for inappropriate reasons.

a. Emanation of the state
b. A Stake in the Outcome
c. A4e
d. Absenteeism

10. _________ is the state of being which occurs when a person, object, or service is no longer wanted even though it may still be in good working order. _________ frequently occurs because a replacement has become available that is superior in one or more aspects. Videotapes making way for DVDs

Technical _________ may occur when a new product or technology supersedes the old, and it becomes preferred to utilize the new technology in place of the old.

a. AAAI
b. A Stake in the Outcome
c. Obsolescence
d. A4e

11. The _________ 1970 is an Act of the United Kingdom Parliament which prohibits any less favourable treatment between men and women in terms of pay and conditions of employment. It came into force on 29 December 1975. The term pay is interpreted in a broad sense to include, on top of wages, things like holidays, pension rights, company perks and some kinds of bonuses.

a. Oncale v. Sundowner Offshore Services
b. Architectural Barriers Act of 1968
c. Australian labour law
d. Equal Pay Act

12. _________s is the science of designing the job, equipment, and workplace to fit the worker. Proper _________ design is necessary to prevent repetitive strain injuries, which can develop over time and can lead to long-term disability.

_________s is concerned with the 'fit' between people and their work.

a. A4e
b. A Stake in the Outcome
c. AAAI
d. Ergonomic

13. _________ are a special type of work behavior that are defined as individual behaviors that are beneficial to the organization and are discretionary, not directly or explicitly recognized by the formal reward system. These behaviors are rather a matter of personal choice, such that their omission are not generally understood as punishable. _________ are thought to have an important impact on the effectiveness and efficiency of work teams and organizations, therefore contributing to the overall productivity of the organization.

a. A4e
b. Organizational citizenship behaviors
c. A Stake in the Outcome
d. AAAI

14. _________ is subcontracting a process, such as product design or manufacturing, to a third-party company. The decision to outsource is often made in the interest of lowering cost or making better use of time and energy costs, redirecting or conserving energy directed at the competencies of a particular business, or to make more efficient use of land, labor, capital, (information) technology and resources. _________ became part of the business lexicon during the 1980s.

a. Unemployment insurance
b. Opinion leadership
c. Operant conditioning
d. Outsourcing

15. _________ is the probability that an individual will keep his or her job; a job with a high level of _________ is such that a person with the job would have a small chance of becoming unemployed.

_________ is dependent on economy, prevailing business conditions, and the individual's personal skills. It has been found that people have more _________ in times of economic expansion and less in times of a recession.

a. Job security
b. Just cause
c. Multiple careers
d. Hygiene factors

16. _________ is unwelcome harassment of a sexual nature, or based upon the receiving party's sex or gender. In some contexts or circumstances, _________ may be illegal. It includes a range of behavior from seemingly mild transgressions and annoyances to actual sexual abuse or sexual assault.

a. Hypernorms
b. 1990 Clean Air Act
c. 28-hour day
d. Sexual harassment

17. The _________ of 1990 (ADA) is the short title of United States (Pub.L. 101-336, 104 Stat. 327, enacted July 26, 1990), codified at 42 U.S.C. Â§ 12101 et seq. It was signed into law on July 26, 1990, by President George H. W. Bush, and later amended with changes effective January 1, 2009. The ADA is a wide-ranging civil rights law that prohibits, under certain circumstances, discrimination based on disability. It affords similar protections against discrimination to Americans with disabilities as the Civil Rights Act of 1964,

a. Australian labour law
b. Americans with Disabilities Act
c. Employment discrimination
d. Equal Pay Act of 1963

18. _________ is an idea in the field of Organizational studies and management which describes the psychology, attitudes, experiences, beliefs and Values (personal and cultural values) of an organization. It has been defined as 'the specific collection of values and norms that are shared by people and groups in an organization and that control the way they interact with each other and with stakeholders outside the organization.'

This definition continues to explain organizational values also known as 'beliefs and ideas about what kinds of goals members of an organization should pursue and ideas about the appropriate kinds or standards of behavior organizational members should use to achieve these goals. From organizational values develop organizational norms, guidelines or expectations that prescribe appropriate kinds of behavior by employees in particular situations and control the behavior of organizational members towards one another.'

_________ is not the same as corporate culture.

a. Organizational development
b. Organizational culture
c. Organizational effectiveness
d. Union shop

19. In operant conditioning, _________ occurs when an event following a response causes an increase in the probability of that response occurring in the future. Response strength can be assessed by measures such as the frequency with which the response is made (for example, a pigeon may peck a key more times in the session), or the speed with which it is made (for example, a rat may run a maze faster.) The environment change contingent upon the response is called a reinforcer.
a. Historiometry
b. Meetings, Incentives, Conferences, and Exhibitions
c. Diminishing Manufacturing Sources and Material Shortages
d. Reinforcement

20. The _________ refers to situations in which students perform better than other students simply because they are expected to do so. The effect is named after George Bernard Shaw's play Pygmalion, in which a professor makes a bet that he can teach a poor flower girl to speak and act like an upper-class lady, and is successful.

The _________ requires a student to internalize the expectations of their superiors.

a. Halo effect
b. Pygmalion effect
c. Confirmation bias
d. Distinction bias

21. _________, in psychology, are goals that are achieved by the contribution and co-operation of two or more people, with individual goals that are normally in opposition to each other, working together.

Muzafer Sherif (1954) performed a study involving a group of boys at a camp that were in opposition to one another, one named Eagles, one named the Rattlers, in a zero-sum situation. The opposing groups had strong negative feelings towards each other, resulting in hostile actions such as 'garbage wars'.

a. 1990 Clean Air Act
b. 28-hour day
c. 33 Strategies of War
d. Superordinate goals

22. Procter is a surname, and may also refer to:

- Bryan Waller Procter (pseud. Barry Cornwall), English poet
- Goodwin Procter, American law firm
- _________, consumer products multinational

.

a. Master and Servant Acts
b. Downstream
c. Strict liability
d. Procter ' Gamble

23. _________ is a system of discipline where the penalties increase upon repeat occurrences.

This term is often used in an employment or human resources context where rather than terminating employees for first or minor infractions, there is a system of escalating responses intended to correct the negative behaviour rather than to punish the employee.

The typical stages of _________ in a workplace are:

1. Counselling or a verbal warning;
2. A written warning;
3. Suspension or demotion; and
4. Termination.

The stage chosen for a particular infraction will depend on a variety of factors that include the severity of the infraction, the previous work history of the employee and how the choice will affect others in the organization.

a. Performance appraisal
b. Human resource management
c. Salary
d. Progressive discipline

24. The _________ captures an expanded spectrum of values and criteria for measuring organizational success: economic, ecological and social. With the ratification of the United Nations and ICLEI _________ standard for urban and community accounting in early 2007, this became the dominant approach to public sector full cost accounting. Similar UN standards apply to natural capital and human capital measurement to assist in measurements required by _________, e.g. the ecoBudget standard for reporting ecological footprint.

a. 28-hour day
b. 33 Strategies of War
c. Triple bottom line
d. 1990 Clean Air Act

25. The _________ is an international organization designed by its founders to supervise and liberalize international trade. The organization officially commenced on 1 January 1995, under the Marrakesh Agreement, succeeding the 1947 General Agreement on Tariffs and Trade (GATT.)

The _________ deals with regulation of trade between participating countries; it provides a framework for negotiating and formalising trade agreements, and a dispute resolution process aimed at enforcing participants' adherence to _________ agreements which are signed by representatives of member governments and ratified by their parliaments.

a. National Institute for Occupational Safety and Health
b. Network planning and design
c. World Trade Organization
d. 1990 Clean Air Act

1. Procter is a surname, and may also refer to:

- Bryan Waller Procter (pseud. Barry Cornwall), English poet
- Goodwin Procter, American law firm
- _________, consumer products multinational

.

a. Procter ' Gamble
b. Master and Servant Acts
c. Downstream
d. Strict liability

2. _________ refers to metrics and measures of output from production processes, per unit of input. Labor _________, for example, is typically measured as a ratio of output per labor-hour, an input. _________ may be conceived of as a metrics of the technical or engineering efficiency of production.
a. Value engineering
b. Remanufacturing
c. Master production schedule
d. Productivity

3. _________ refers to a range of skills, tools, and techniques used to manage time when accomplishing specific tasks, projects and goals. This set encompass a wide scope of activities, and these include planning, allocating, setting goals, delegation, analysis of time spent, monitoring, organizing, scheduling, and prioritizing. Initially _________ referred to just business or work activities, but eventually the term broadened to include personal activities also.
a. Formula for Change
b. Cash cow
c. Time management
d. Voice of the customer

4. _________ is a set of values based on hard work and diligence. It is also a belief in the moral benefit of work and its ability to enhance character. An example would be the Protestant _________.
a. 1990 Clean Air Act
b. 33 Strategies of War
c. Work ethic
d. 28-hour day

5. _________ is one of the managerial functions like planning, organizing, staffing and directing. It is an important function because it helps to check the errors and to take the corrective action so that deviation from standards are minimized and stated goals of the organization are achieved in desired manner.According to modern concepts, _________ is a foreseeing action whereas earlier concept of _________ was used only when errors were detected. _________ in management means setting standards, measuring actual performance and taking corrective action.
   a. Schedule of reinforcement
   b. Control
   c. Turnover
   d. Decision tree pruning

6. The _________, 5 U.S.C. Â§ 552a, establishes a code of fair information practices that governs the collection, maintenance, use, and dissemination of personally identifiable information about individuals that is maintained in systems of records by federal agencies. A system of records is a group of records under the control of an agency from which information is retrieved by the name of the individual or by some identifier assigned to the individual.
   a. Privacy Act of 1974
   b. Negligence
   c. Personal Responsibility and Work Opportunity Reconciliation Act
   d. No-FEAR Act

7. _________ is a type of trade policy that allows traders to act and transact without interference from government. Thus, the policy permits trading partners mutual gains from trade, with goods and services produced according to the theory of comparative advantage.

Under a _________ policy, prices are a reflection of true supply and demand, and are the sole determinant of resource allocation.

   a. 33 Strategies of War
   b. 1990 Clean Air Act
   c. Free Trade
   d. 28-hour day

8. _________ is a designated group of countries that have agreed to eliminate tariffs, quotas and preferences on most (if not all) goods and services traded between them. It can be considered the second stage of economic integration. Countries choose this kind of economic integration form if their economical structures are complementary.
   a. 28-hour day
   b. Free trade area
   c. 1990 Clean Air Act
   d. 33 Strategies of War

9. _________ is a term in psychology which refers to a person's belief about what causes the good or bad results in his or her life, either in general or in a specific area such as health or academics. Understanding of the concept was developed by Julian B. Rotter in 1954, and has since become an important aspect of personality studies.

_________ refers to the extent to which individuals believe that they can control events that affect them.

a. Social loafing
b. Self-enhancement
c. Locus of control
d. Machiavellianism

10. _________ is 'a form of interrole conflict in which the role pressures from the work and family domains are mutually incompatible in some respect. That is participation in the work (family) role is made more difficult by virtue of participation in the family (work) role' (Greenhaus ' Beutell, 1985, p.77.) Conflict between work and family is important for organizations and individuals because it is linked to negative consequences.

a. 28-hour day
b. 33 Strategies of War
c. 1990 Clean Air Act
d. Work-family conflict

11. The _________ 1970 is an Act of the United Kingdom Parliament which prohibits any less favourable treatment between men and women in terms of pay and conditions of employment. It came into force on 29 December 1975. The term pay is interpreted in a broad sense to include, on top of wages, things like holidays, pension rights, company perks and some kinds of bonuses.

a. Oncale v. Sundowner Offshore Services
b. Australian labour law
c. Equal Pay Act
d. Architectural Barriers Act of 1968

12. _________ is a strategic planning method used to evaluate the Strengths, Weaknesses, Opportunities, and Threats involved in a project or in a business venture. It involves specifying the objective of the business venture or project and identifying the internal and external factors that are favorable and unfavorable to achieving that objective. The technique is credited to Albert Humphrey, who led a convention at Stanford University in the 1960s and 1970s using data from Fortune 500 companies.

a. Market share
b. Corporate image
c. SWOT analysis
d. Marketing

Chapter 1

1. d	2. d	3. d	4. d	5. d	6. d	7. c	8. d	9. d	10. d
11. a	12. a	13. d	14. a	15. b	16. d	17. d	18. d	19. d	20. b
21. d	22. d	23. d	24. d	25. a	26. a	27. c	28. d		

Chapter 2

1. d	2. b	3. b	4. d	5. d	6. d	7. a	8. b	9. b	10. a
11. a	12. a	13. b	14. a	15. d	16. d	17. d	18. c	19. d	20. d
21. d	22. c	23. d	24. c						

Chapter 3

1. b	2. b	3. a	4. c	5. d	6. b	7. d	8. d	9. d	10. d
11. b	12. a	13. a	14. c						

Chapter 4

1. d	2. a	3. a	4. d	5. d	6. b	7. d	8. d	9. b	10. d
11. b	12. d	13. c	14. b						

Chapter 5

1. d	2. d	3. c	4. d	5. b	6. a	7. a	8. c	9. d	10. b
11. d	12. a	13. b	14. c	15. c	16. a				

Chapter 6

1. d	2. a	3. d	4. c	5. d	6. c	7. a	8. a	9. d	10. a
11. d	12. d								

Chapter 7

1. d	2. b	3. d	4. d	5. d	6. b	7. d	8. a	9. d	10. a
11. c	12. d	13. c	14. d	15. d	16. b	17. d	18. d	19. d	20. d
21. d	22. c	23. d	24. d	25. d	26. d	27. d			

Chapter 8

1. d	2. b	3. d	4. d	5. d	6. d	7. a	8. b	9. b	10. c
11. d	12. b	13. b	14. b	15. d	16. d	17. b	18. a	19. c	20. b
21. d	22. d	23. d	24. d	25. d	26. d	27. d	28. b	29. d	

Chapter 9

1. b	2. b	3. d	4. d	5. a	6. d	7. b	8. b	9. d	10. c
11. d	12. d	13. d	14. d	15. a	16. a	17. c	18. b	19. a	20. b
21. d	22. b	23. d	24. d	25. d					

Chapter 10

1. b	2. d	3. b	4. b	5. d	6. c	7. d	8. b	9. a	10. c
11. d	12. c	13. c	14. c	15. d	16. a				

Chapter 11

1. d	2. c	3. c	4. d	5. d	6. d	7. b	8. d	9. a	10. d
11. d	12. d	13. b	14. c	15. d	16. b	17. a	18. a	19. d	20. d

Chapter 12

1. b	2. d	3. d	4. a	5. d	6. d	7. a	8. a	9. b	10. c
11. b	12. d	13. d	14. c	15. a					

Chapter 13

1. d	2. d	3. c	4. d	5. a	6. d	7. d	8. d	9. a	10. b
11. b	12. a	13. d	14. a	15. d	16. a	17. a	18. a	19. b	20. d
21. d	22. a	23. c							

Chapter 14

1. d	2. b	3. d	4. c	5. a	6. d	7. a	8. c	9. d	10. d
11. d	12. c	13. a	14. d	15. c					

Chapter 15

1. d	2. a	3. d	4. b	5. d	6. d	7. c	8. c	9. d	10. a
11. d	12. d	13. d	14. a	15. a	16. c	17. d	18. d	19. d	20. a
21. b	22. a	23. d	24. d	25. a	26. d	27. d	28. b	29. c	30. d
31. b	32. d	33. d							

Chapter 16

1. c	2. a	3. d	4. d	5. b	6. a	7. d	8. b	9. d	10. c
11. d	12. d	13. b	14. d	15. a	16. d	17. b	18. b	19. d	20. b
21. d	22. d	23. d	24. c	25. c					

Chapter 17

1. a	2. d	3. c	4. c	5. b	6. a	7. c	8. b	9. c	10. d
11. c	12. c								

www.ingramcontent.com/pod-product-compliance
Lightning Source LLC
Chambersburg PA
CBHW082051230426
43670CB00016B/2857
* 9 7 8 1 4 2 8 8 7 2 4 4 8 *